CYCLING

SOLO

CYCLING SOLO

SOLO

Ireland to Istanbul

Hazel Edwards and Trevelyan Quest Edwards

Published by Brolga Publishing Pty Ltd
ABN 46 063 962 443
PO Box 12544
A'Beckett St, VIC, 8006
Australia
email: markzocchi@brolgapublishing.com.au

National Library of Australia
Cataloguing-in-Publication data

Edwards, Trevelyan Quest, 1975–.
Cycling Solo : Ireland to Istanbul

ISBN 9781920785925
ISBN 1920785922

1. Edwards, Trevelyan Quest, 1975– - Travel - Europe.
2. Cycling - Europe
3. Camping - Europe
4. Europe - Description and travel
I. Edwards, Hazel, 1945–
II. Title

914.0456

Printed in Singapore
Cover by David Khan
Designed and typeset by Diana Evans

Would you like to be published?

National booktrade distribution through Pan Macmillan
bepublished@brolgapublishing.com.au

Blog Entries

Dublin Post Office

My mobile rang.

"Would you know where Trevelyan Edwards might be?" asked a pleasant Irish male voice. "This is Dublin Post Office. We have found his lost rucksack which was reported lost a year ago. We would like to post it to him."

Even for a family of agnostics, this was a postal miracle, the day before St Patrick's Day. Apparently my business card had been in my son's backpack which had been lost in the Irish postal system for the entire time he had been cycling from Ireland to Istanbul and beyond. This rucksack, as the Irish called it, contained his back-up documents, photos and clothes and had been especially registered, but still lost.

"He's back working in Darwin. We're in Melbourne, Australia. I'm sure he'll be delighted to hear from you."

For a family, it's reassuring to feel that there are electronic connections, mobile, email and blogging: even if they are belated back -ups, through different time and language zones or occasionally off the map or lost in a postal system!

"Blogging" is mind-mapping, electronically recorded in the moment at Internet cafes.

So this is a solo cyclist's quest with later editing, detours and additions.

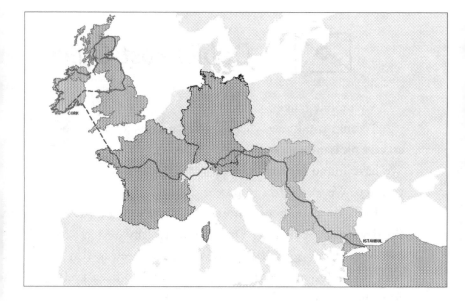

NAME:	Trevelyan Quest Edwards
AGE:	29
OCCUPATION:	Cartographer
TRANSPORT:	Mountain Bike
HEIGHT:	187 cm
WEIGHT:	5 kilos less at end of cycling quest
DISTANCE:	Ireland to Istanbul – over 9,000 kilometres plus detours but difficult to be accurate as bike computer failed early.
CYCLING TIME:	Five months

 *Detours*

The highlight of this trip was the freedom of travelling on a bike and being able to camp wherever I could find a reclusive clearing, preferably next to a river for washing and cooking. I carried everything else I needed. Waking up without a clue of where I'd be the next night except that it would be within 150 kilometres was my kind of blissful traveling.

Often I was lost – but I was found. No, I wasn't 'born again' in the religious sense, I was acquiring a nomadic mindset. I didn't wear a watch, but I had a compass. Getting lost in Eastern Europe didn't hold the same fears as getting lost in the Northern Territory (where I live).

For example, when buying my THIRD map in Sofia, I realised that I still couldn't work out which way to get onto the E8 and out of town. The main problem was that all my maps (a tourist guide to highlights, a map of Bulgaria and a map of Sofia) were in the English alphabet and the signs I was looking at were in Cyrillic – all Greek to me.

In the end, it really didn't matter. I knew all I had to do was head east southeast. I had enough food and drinking water for two days on my bike and there was enough light to cycle out of the city and find somewhere to pitch the tent. Everything important (food, shelter, water) was set and if I did get lost, it was never long before I would come across a village and the only thing that would be lost was a bit of time.

Time was the only thing that mattered. Time to have a yarn. Time to gesticulate and explain that I wasn't Austrian, "Nien spreche sie Deutsche," do a skippy dance and say, "Syderneey" and "Melerburn" umpteen times. Time to explain that I wasn't really from Sydney but, oh well, it didn't matter and by the way this coffee is great but how do you say milk in your language?

At the start, Irish people took pity on the stupid bloke on a bike who was wet and frozen and brought their pragmatism to my proposed journey.

"Och aye, Istanbul's a long way laddie, you should fly."

"Well, I want to see what's in between."

"Drive then."

"I can't afford that."

"Train."

"Trains only go to the cities and they're too expensive."

"Bus then."

I have an aversion to buses too. Mate, I've spent days on them travelling around Oz and I don't think I could handle Contiki.

"Well then laddie, if you don't want to drive, and you want to go on two wheels, a motorbike's your answer."

I didn't have much money; I had time and didn't mind roughing it. So a deadly treadly was my way.

Extraordinary, ordinary people went out of their way to direct me or offer hospitality. That's why I've edited my former blog notes to pay credit to those who help lone, strange travellers, like me.

Why Blog?

I guess I am my namesake. 'Quest' is my real middle name. And my 'real' job back in Darwin is as a cartographer. I'm a bit of a dreamer but only a bit because I try to set goals, especially for the best dreams. I'm currently following one of my longest held dreams by travelling around the world and at the moment am stuck in Ireland kitting out a mountain bike with world domination in sight. I'm going to cycle alone from Ireland to Istanbul and keep a blog en route as my media journal of choice.

Hopefully, there won't be any junk e-mail to deal with on the blog site 'cos I've had my fill of great stock options, herbal Viagra and people I've never heard of 'wanting to meet me'.

With bulk e-mails I would have spent too much time replying to separate people, but a blog is a stand alone medium, which saves time and my family will know where I am, or where I was when I wrote the last entry. Blogging will allow me to turn up to an Internet café with story in tow and just write straight away without distractions. After fulfilling that initial creative rush, I can then get more personal and answer e-mails directly. It will also be a record, where my family and friends can leave comments.

Ok… enough justification, now for a status update. Back to the start of this quest, the beginning of the blog…

 *Dublin*

Monday April 18, 2005

Well, I've finally made it. Yesterday morning I caught the ferry over from Hollyhead and set my feet on the green, green grass of Ireland. Well, not really. It was more like I set my feet on the concrete walkway of Dublin Harbour, but the weather was wet and windy so if I had closed my eyes then I'm sure undulating hills, grass and stone walls would have appeared before me.

Didn't get much sleep on the bus/ferry trip over but that didn't matter because I was pretty excited about my current location. Ireland has been of personal Celtic interest for years. I quickly found a backpackers to dump my gear at and then decided to go for a wander. Dublin – what a city. There were monuments, references to James Joyce, old buildings and pubs everywhere. I began walking in a pretty myopic fashion and ended up grabbing a map after I had crossed an intersection for the third time.

First Map

The Dublin map was free, very colourful and I was professionally impressed with its layout. The tourist sites had an image of the building on the map, which meant it was pretty easy to orientate myself as every block or so there was a distinctive site to recognise.

From the map, I was near City Hall so I expected that it would be like other city halls that I'd visited – more of a tourist bureau than anything else. Once I had entered though, I found out that it was practically a museum in its own right. There were historical monuments in situ, excellent (I mean really comprehensive) information booklets that described the monuments and their meanings. Downstairs there was one of the best outlays of a city I had ever seen. There were historical, religious and engineering timelines of Dublin, how they interrelated and the people that had made it happen. Here was a city that was proud of itself.

Once I had finished my tour of City Hall, I found that there was going to be a musical recital soon. It was free, so of course I was interested.

 *Musical Ticks*

My dad (a Wagnerian opera fan) is going to read these next words in horror because I don't know what you call a group that all play string instruments and suffer from nervous ticks.

There were 10 of them – a string tenet? They had 6 violins, 2 violas? and 2 cellos. The music was great. A lot of it sounded familiar although I only recognised Pachebel's 'Canon'. It was probably a mix of classical greatest hits judging by how the audience reacted after the first few bars of each piece.

The musicians seemed to be having a good time although the front girls were having a hard time keeping straight faces. They were either sharing a private joke or laughing at the facial contortions of one of the blokes playing a viola. He was obviously concentrating intently and deeply immersed in his task. I think he must practice solo a lot – without any mirrors.

Once the recital had finished, I went off to the next big building on my map, Christ Church Cathedral. They made me pay on entry, something I was hesitant to do after having seen so much for free already, but I relented. The donation boxes scattered around the cathedral weren't bothered by my presence though.

 # Bells Ringing, Ringing, Ringing

As I walked around I saw a big group gathering at one end and so I went to investigate. They were going up to the belfry. Dutifully tagging along, it turned out that this group was going to be entertained by the ringing of the bells.

Christ Church Cathedral has more bells in it than any other cathedral in the world although they don't have enough trained bell ringers to ring them all. Ringing a bell didn't look too hard to me – you pull a rope, catch it and pull it again – but I was soon suitably impressed by the fervour of the head bell ringer. This was an exact science and a complicated musical art form to boot.

I think the head ringer got a bit too excited in his displays because we were stuck up there for a long time as he showed us different types of bells, different ringing combinations, different strengths of the ringings etc. The audience didn't help out as they fuelled the fervour by asking pertinent questions. I began wondering how often the head ringer was allowed to ring the bells as he wasn't showing any desire to stop ringing them and I was sure that the people who lived next to the church must have had mixed feelings towards the loud bells. I asked him how often they were allowed to ring the bells.

"Friday for practice and on Sunday."

Willing to show my religious knowledge, I said, "Sunday is for the calling to mass?"

"Errr no!" he said, eyeing me suspiciously. "The Catholics have Mass, we are the ****" (I can't remember which Christian religion it was but it wasn't Catholic.)

I had the grace to blush violently and blubber, "Oh God, whoops, I mean sorry, hell, I've only been here for a day and I'm from Australia."

The head ringer didn't talk to me after that and we finished up the tour pretty soon. I thought to myself: 'Not bad, 12 hours in Ireland and I've already managed to offend religious sensibilities, blaspheme in a cathedral and tarnished my nation's image in the eyes of bell ringers.' I found out later that the cathedral had been Catholic 400 years ago, so I guess I'm just half a millennium behind the times.

Cultured out, I walked past a pub and had a Guinness… cool. Now I knew what the fuss was about. Dublin Guinness was a lot better than Darwin Guinness.

Today was also the All Ireland Hurling Final which I had been looking forward to seeing and maybe playing, as it is the local sport. Unfortunately, that final game signalled the end of the season for hurling so I was going to have to find another sport to play during the off-season. All good. That pretty much concluded my first Irish day.

←→

Cycling Plans coming soon but a few local observations first.

 # *Ireland Culture*

Apart from the obvious climatic differences between Ireland and Darwin, beer consumption is on a par. In Darwin, you drink because it's hot and the beers are cold. In Ireland, you drink because the weather's cold and the pubs are warm.

Another similarity with Darwin is the Irish lack of haste. Whether due to excessive consumption of alcohol or other reasons, it can be a bit infuriating when you are waiting for a response to job enquiries. Even though I plan to live simply, I need to fund my cycling tour, so a temporary job is essential. After sending out heaps of job applications and CVs, I was left in a weird state of limbo. Were the employers interested? Had the job gone? One job enquiry I sent out took three weeks to get back and ask for my CV. Ahh, it almost feels like home.

Face to face communication can also be a problem. The local nomadic group are called 'Travellers' which is the PC (politically correct) term, and I have about as much hope understanding them as I do a full blooded Aboriginal back home. Whether they are speaking with a full accent, in Gaelic, or some form of pig English, all I can do is smile and shake my shoulders. I put on my best accent and say, "Je ne comprehend pas." I've worked out that this is probably the best phrase when you want to be left alone because although it's a made up phrase it implies 'don't understand' and people don't have a clue what language it is so they move onto easier game. On the whole though, I can communicate with most of the locals after I get them to slow down and repeat what they've said.

↔

In a surprising turn of efficiency I had an interview within five days of my enquiry and was notified of my employment on the same day. The interview itself was fairly relaxed but when they asked the question: "Do you think there will be any difference between dealing with American customers and Irish ones?" I had to bite my tongue. The first thought that came to my head was, American clients are probably sober. My second thought was I could probably understand an American better. After a pause to gather my thoughts, the answer came to me.

"American customers are probably quite demanding when they ask for assistance as they live in a technologically advanced society and expect fairly instantaneous gratification." (That and they're probably sober.)

↔

So I have managed to get a temporary three month contract with Apple at their call centre in Cork. I have two weeks paid training from nine to five and then two and a half months of night shift work. This should be enough for me to finally get the bike organised, get a house, a bank account (impossible without a permanent address) and quit smoking (impossible in a backpackers). Ireland's financial year runs

concurrently with its calendar year and any tax in the next two and a half months should be refunded and will part fund my trip. I need to earn as much as possible before starting to cycle from Ireland to Istanbul.

Cold, Wet and Unfashionable

In answer to a number of queries I've received... I'm still alive. Only just though as the Arctic winds, ice, sleet and snow have threatened to freeze my tropically conditioned constitution. That and the ever apparent danger of slipping on the massive amounts of dog poo that populate the streets of Cork means my obituary may read:

"Trevelyan killed after sliding down Patrick Hill on one foot. Sniffer dogs confused but happy."

Westerly wind is cold. Northerly wind is cold. Sometimes there is a south easterly and it is... well... Cold. To prove how cold it is, they have one of those big coke stands that have a clock and a digital thermometer on it. I think the thermometer only has room for a single digit because a second number would be a waste of space. Still, the cold does have some advantages. You can wear lots of clothes and because you don't sweat at all, you can wear the same clothes over and over again in different combinations. So far

I have been able to wear one shirt five times, three times as an undershirt, once as a top shirt and once as earmuffs under my beanie.

Beanies are great. Apparently you lose 70 per cent of your body heat through your head, and when you have no hair that number at least trebles. Beanies reverse that trend and I never leave home without my now, albeit a little smelly, beanie. When clothes become an essential survival item, you begin to notice what everyone else wears. Being the fashion stalwart you all know that I am, I have broken the locals into three groups – Fashionable, Working and the Rest.

The Rest (to which I belong) wear lots of clothes, look like Michelin men and walk around happy and a bit ungainly. Working people can be broken into two groups – construction and professional. Construction people look very unhappy in their fluorescent yellow bibs and barely adequate clothing as they go about their business tearing up anything nailed down in order to make Cork the Cultural Capital of Europe...

Business people breeze past in their tailored uniforms and umbrellas looking quite smug as they mingle with the masses on the street for their ten minutes of cardiovascular workout.

Now for my favorite group... the Fashionable. I don't want to appear ignorant, but what sort of survival value do woven ponchos have? I mean, girls, it's Arctic temperature, so, long boots, mini skirt and boob tube are all fine as long as you have some sort of jacket to maintain an outer barrier of warmth. How is a poncho which has less wool than my socks, going to keep you warm? That said, the poncho obviously has some sort of indiscernible effect as the local girls swear by them.

My next favorite item of clothing, which is a lot more practical, is the down jacket. For all those Darwinites out there, a down-filled jacket looks like a life jacket. White seems to be the colour of choice and unlike ponchos, down jackets are unisexual. I have spied a number of matching jackets. I am almost a bit envious because they look quite warm, but… leather jackets abound and if I ever have the opportunity to scale the fashion ladder, it will be courtesy of a leather jacket. You can tell a true 'Corker' by their worn leather jacket, woollen underlay, clenched teeth and icicles in their facial growth.

Me, I have a cold threshold and once I reach it I stagger back to the hostel, which has a sauna in the basement. I think I am the only person who uses it, but that sauna is to me a portal back to Darwin, back to heat, sweat and a thing called circulation.

Cold, wet and unfashionable, Trev.

↔

Today I was at a tranquil place the 'Rock of Cashel'. Tranquil because when the gale wind blew across the exposed peak, my brain achieved a Nirvana state as it froze. The place itself was beautiful but I don't think I gave it adequate attention as I half jogged around the perimeter. At least I have learned that in future when I walk more than ten minutes from shelter I have to have adequate survival resources to see me through any blizzard.

Until the bike is sorted (having trouble getting panniers) I have hired a car so that I can visit as many frozen relics as possible, without becoming one.

The lady at the car agency looked a bit apprehensive when she saw my well worn bags and backpacker apparel but I soon put her mind at ease with beguiling charm and a credit card. What her reaction was when I drove out, I'm not sure because I was too busy trying to unstall the car and turn off the windscreen wipers and high beam. Why do the French have to make cars? The indicators are on the wrong side, they have lots of useless weird gadgets and the speedo is in miles.

After a while I started to get used to my Peugeot and began marvelling at Irish road customs. They didn't seem to have any speed indicators on the road except for when you entered a town and had to drop to thirty. However they had lots of signs warning about the risks of speeding and the penalties involved which I dutifully took note of – and then ignored – because I had no idea of how fast I was allowed to be travelling.

The general rule of driving seems to be – the wider the road, the slower you go. If you are on a three lane motorway (freeway), then 50 mph seems to be the going rate. If you are on a narrow, pothole filled, stonewall encased byroad then the sky is the limit. Irish drivers are very courteous and let you through which is a good thing because you don't want to meet them coming the other way.

Internal sport aside, I think the Irish are quite happy to be bridesmaids. In fact, I think they prefer to run second than to be the arrogant first at anything. In Dublin I saw numerous references to it being secondary to London. The second biggest, the second to do this etc… It's almost like they want to say, "Aye we're good but them mob…" I mused over this after I pulled into a small town last night that proudly displayed the fact that they were the silver medalist in the tidy town contest. I used the picnic area to cook my meal and saw a pile of junk that the last occupant had strewn about. After much deliberation I decided to put the rubbish in the bin and quickly drove away in case the locals noticed that I might have pushed them into gold medal contention.

Tomorrow it's off to the Blarney Stone to get the gift of the gab and maybe a coldsore. Who knows what blarney could be in the next report.

Great Blasket and Early Gaelic Autobiographies

Just a quick note as I am waiting for my laundry to wash and this is a pretty expensive Internet café.

I've camped in some unusual places – in a graveyard at Blarney, on a beach at Dingle, and on a pier in Galway. There aren't many parks and very few national parks in Ireland so trying to find a place to pull over and crash can be a bit of a mission sometimes. Last night in Galway the pier had two signs – one had a tent crossed out and the other with a caravan crossed out. Seeing as how I wasn't sleeping in either, I reasoned that I wasn't disobeying the signs and I had a good night's sleep.

One highlight has been Blasket Centre, a museum in the deep south west that tells the story of the village on Great Blasket Island which had pretty much maintained its medieval lifestyle up to 60 odd years ago when it was evacu-ated. Since they had maintained their Gaelic language and oral traditions, the island became of interest to scholars last century as one of the few places where the Irish language had-n't been tainted by English. Visiting scholars encouraged the Islanders to write down their autobiographies and folk lore.

This has resulted in a small collection of books that tell the story of real village life from a first person perspective. (A bit like a blog really!) Almost scary reading some of these books and thinking that was the mindset of much of Ireland for most of its history. Religion dominated and life was a hard struggle for those people.

Anyway got to go as the laundry should be dry, to be sure, to be sure…

←→

Returned the car. I've now bought a bike, a decent one too which is a big step up from the deathtraps I used to ride around Darwin. I've been acquiring the gear I need for the big cycle tour and for training have been riding home in the early hours. Cold!

Since I bought the bike, the weather has deteriorated rapidly so I have now christened the bike 'Stormbringer'. Last night I even got to ride home in snow… Awesome.

 # *Memories of Corkers*

Cork has been a memorable town (easier to get a job than Dublin) and some of the best memories are:

✓ Cork overwhelms with its number of pubs. They are literally everywhere and some big pubs are even conglomerates of multiple small pubs with the dividing walls knocked out. Drinking is more than a social outing, it's a source of cultural spirit and shelter with lots of impromptu music and singing.

✓ A White Christmas. Not only that, but my first snow ever. Wow, I never knew that snow was so cold and making a snow man would freeze your fingers. Snow fights rule too, especially if you have a height and size advantage and a throwing arm developed from junior cricket years.

✓ Corkonians (or Corkers behind their back). Ahh the Irish, friendly, lovable but practically impossible to understand. There is so much to love about the Irish, their passionate hatred for the English, their great pubs, their awesome stouts, their music, their lackadaisical attitude: all good. However, they do have a rather pessimistic attitude to life, probably due to the 800 years of English oppression that invariably creeps into any conversation. Maybe the weather is also a factor, as from my experience so far, it has been dark, wet and cold. In all though, it can get a little repetitive when you've heard the same story for the umpteenth time.

✔ I saw a big exhibition on James Joyce at the national library so I finally forked out to buy a copy of Ulysses to see what all the fuss is about. So far (100 pages) – I can understand why people enjoy his prose, he can be quite poetic, but the book itself seems to be pretty garbled infatuation. Still, it's early days and the book is supposed to be one of the greatest ever written so I will persevere.

✔ The beer... Mmmm pub culture, despite working nights and being a teetotaler during the week, it is nice to be able to drink real Guinness: Murphy's, Kilkenny etc... on weekends. There really is no contest between the stouts here and the imposters back home in Darwin.

✗ The rubbish. Mate.... Anyone would think that after thousands of years of settlement they would have a decent rubbish collection system. Unfortunately no! Cork had just introduced a pay per pick up system when I arrived which meant that our rubbish stopped being collected. After four months of chasing the city council, the landlord and even checking the legal situation (renters have practically no rights in Eire), I finally got the rubbish collected again. For a while though, there was a big heap of rubbish out the back and it was only due to some illegal rubbish-runs late at night that the pile didn't get out of hand.

↔

Re: Cycling Plans coming soon.

 # Cycling Plans

I've been constantly delayed in setting off. The main problem is that I've had a fair bit of trouble getting the bike kitted out in preparation for the trip. Panniers, panniers, panniers.

Firstly, the bloke in Dublin who was going to send me some rear panniers and a rack kept forgetting to send them. Then, the desperation order that I put through to get rear panniers, a rack and a low rider fell through, due to lack of stock. In the end, I spent a couple of days searching all the Cork bike stores in order to find the equipment. Unfortunately, I couldn't find any equipment that I really needed but after some logistical nightmares, and a lot of ocky straps, I finally worked out a way to stick all my camping gear on the bike.

➤ Email From Home

Have you left Ireland yet?

No, I haven't left yet. Sent all my superfluous gear to my mate Mark in Newcastle (UK) so if the worst case scenario happens (i.e. my bike gets stolen) then he can mail me my backpack and at least I will have some clothes, money and photocopies of documents. So, I'm now fully packed, have vacated my house and am spending a weekend in Cork as a final fling... Bring on the road and the four months of gorgeous sunshine that will now befall Europe. Really looking forward to this trip, it's the biggest mission I've ever undertaken.

 # Saddle-sore

Two days in and saddle-sore already...

I am writing these words in Kenmare on the verge of the Ring of Kerry. My initial forays into the depths of Western Ireland have been a varied experience. I knew that I was going

to suffer over the first week, but still, I was kind of hoping for some nice weather to ease me into it.

First Cycling Day

After several ineffectual attempts to work a route out, I decided to head west. West was good as it brought me to the River Lee which I was able to follow for the whole day. I started to cheer up and was grinding the miles out.

Thought to myself, 'What a lovely day. A bit cold but that makes exercise easier.'

Three minutes later it started to rain. Got jacket out and kept going.

'Hmm,' I pondered. 'At least the rain's not too heavy.'

Rain started to lash.

At least I now know that my gear is all waterproof except for the cycle computer that managed to die after 60 kilometres. From then on, I was never sure of my mileage and people always ask, "How far have you travelled?"

The cycling was pretty miserable as I could never really get warm or dry, but at least the rain finished before I broke camp. And what a camp it was. Around 6 p.m. I'd had enough punishment so I thought I would check out Guougane Barra Forest Park. It turned out to be a great place for a stopover.

There was a gorgeous, holy site on an island which

appeared to be a pilgrimage site as it had some fairly complicated instructions full of praises and Hail Marys. While I was
leaving, a minibus of nuns turned up complete with travelling habit. The setting of the church and the obvious care
with which it was maintained, meant that it was probably the
prettiest church I'd ever seen and if I was religious, I would
want to pray there. The information board stated that the site
was lit up at night so I went back once it was dark with
romantic hopes of 'highlighting backlight' and 'reflecting
lights' only to find out that it was lit up with street light
hybrids. Still I didn't begrudge them that, as it was very cute.

My campsite was great too, isolated, park seats, serviced
by a fast running creek and framed by an imposing gorge. In
all, I woke up reinvigorated and had forgotten all about the
rain…

↔

Rain. Hmm. Summer soon. It can't come quick enough.
In all, not too bad a day cycling. Less rain than yesterday, but
it definitely felt a lot colder. Getting a bit sore in the saddle
early on but I readjusted the seat and now it feels a lot better.
I stopped for lunch in a small town and as I couldn't feel my
fingers, I decided to go into the pub to warm up. I remembered reading somewhere that alcohol contains large
amounts of energy, so with that thought in mind I bought a
Murphy's and slowly drank it by the heater.

Next stage was a hill crossing, which I was halfway up
when suddenly the sun appeared. Not only that but a tailwind kicked up.

'Awesome,' I thought. 'All that bad weather is behind
me.'

Almost as suddenly the sun disappeared and the tailwind increased into a gale and changed direction by 180 degrees. Still, the downhill was fun and I have now decided to cycle without thinking, which as all the people who know me will know, is not a huge effort on my part.

←→

Getting to Kenmare took a lot more out of me than I thought. That and my body is still on nightshift. I eventually found a nice camp spot about 10 kilometres southwest of Kenmare hidden from the road and overlooking Kenmare Bay. I didn't bother cooking dinner, just flaked out. Fourteen hours later woke to a beautiful sunny day but seeing as how it was already half gone (plus I guessed it would take me about two hours to pack) I decided to have a day off.

Golf

I had seen a golf course just before my campsite and the Lonely Planet stated that it cost $20 for a round, so I thought 'Why not?'

Unfortunately, the golf course the Lonely Planet was talking about was on the other side of town (20 kilometres away) and I had blundered onto one of the championship courses. Eighty dollars for 18 holes. Still, I was in a golfing mood, so I ended up playing 9 holes.

The course was a little tougher than the Gardens Course back in the Territory and it had an absolute stunning view over the bay. I won't bore you with the details of my triple and quadruple bogies… Instead I'll tell you about my almost eagle birdie that I hit on the fifth. Amazingly I hit an arrow straight driver and then a perfect 5 wood onto the green. Had a 15 metre putt for eagle and it was on line but fell short by about 30 centimetres.

That and getting to ring a big bell at the bottom of a hidden dogleg (to allow the next people to tee off) even though there was no-one behind me, made my round. The changing rooms at the course had to be seen to be believed so I availed myself of a very long soap and hot shower which was incomparable to that morning's dip in Kerry Bay.

↔

Another long sleep. That seems to be my lot now. Got all packed up and headed off along the Ring. The weather was sunny and I was in a good mood. My knee, which had been hurting a bit on the first couple of days, wasn't giving me any bother so the only slight annoyance was a squeaking noise which I think is the bolts on the rear rack working themselves loose (which they do over the course of a day). First tourist attraction – a big round fort.

#\$@%!! – I just lost the rest of my post and the post office is closing. I'll finish this off another time.

↔

Unfortunately I lost around two-thirds of the last post. You'll just have to take my word for it that it was extremely witty and full of amazing adventure. I'll try to remember as much as possible but it'll pale in comparison to the original…

First tourist attraction – a big round fort, which as big round forts tend to be, was located at the top of a hilly valley. Thank goodness that I've spent the last three months cycling up Military and Holly Hills to and from the night shift as Kerry seems to be built on an angle, either up or down.

The stone fort was impressive – very impressive – so I decided to go into the big round fort 'Experience' (the fort does have a name but it escapes me). The 'Experience' comprised of a 10 minute video saying that they weren't sure exactly what the fort was used for but there were many ways it could have been used and if they excavated it then there was a chance they would be able to make a better guess but that they could never be exactly sure of its use. An hour later when I was cycling around a particularly exposed mountain pass, I knew exactly what it was built for – a wind barrier.

At the top of that climb, I came across another monument to Mary. There are some really good religious monuments scattered around the countryside. Mostly they are to Mary but some are of the crucifixion. There is invariably a statue but generally the best part of the monument is the way in which the statue has been framed, sometimes in a very artistic manner. This monument was stonewalled fenced with a gravel cross as the walkway, a feature I didn't catch until I stepped back to take a photo… Nice.

I had camped about a half hour outside Waterville (where according to the Lonely Planet, a round of golf costs $120) and had my customary 10-plus hours sleep. Woke up cold and wet. Spent most of the day in the tent reading and writing but journeyed out for a food and Internet run.

←→

Good weather… awesome. Woke up fresh and eager and packed ASAP. Set off full of beans but within half an hour had found an artists' retreat at Ballinskellig, so spent a fair part of the morning looking through the gallery and drinking coffee. The lady who made the coffee was extremely apologetic that the milk had lumps in it despite my assurances it was okay. I'm getting a bit worried that my camping mentality is taking over because when I saw the lumps, initially I was thinking that the coagulated milk might contain some of the antioxidants that yoghurt has and I kept pouring. Then this woman wanted to throw it away. Imagine her thinking that my protests were out of politeness!

 *Skellig Chilli Whisky Chocolate*

After my free coffee, I was ready to blitz the Skellig Ring. Rode some customary undulations and came across a chocolate factory in the middle of nowhere. There were no customers there so I had a fairly long chat with the owner who turned out to be an IT guy who had worked throughout Asia and Australia. As we talked, he let me sample pretty much everything they made.

I have to say that if you ever get a chance to buy/try the

Skellig factory chilli whisky chocolate then do. It is (for want of a better word) divine. The first take is chocolate, then whisky and then it almost effortlessly blends into the chilli which complements the whisky no end. The owner warned me about the upcoming hill, but wired with caffeine and cocoa, I was ready for anything.

A quarter of the way up – coffee was well gone. Cocoa hung in there a bit longer but in the end it was sheer bloody mindedness that got me up that hill without stopping. I wasn't going to let it break me and with my first legitimate use of the 'granny gear' (lowest possible gear combination for our non cyclist readers) I made it through. After that it was a coast down to Portmagee.

Now I had read a lot about the Skellig Islands and it was highlighted as a 'must-do', however the boats had already berthed for the day so I explored Valencia Island (including doing a bit of mountain biking to convince myself why I was

Ring of Skellig

on one instead of a touring bike). I then went to the Skellig Experience (a bit of a trend happening here) which was a lot more comprehensive and conclusive about the uses of the island than the round fort experience.

As the boats weren't setting out until 11 a.m. the next day (and there was no guarantee that they would leave then), I decided to head for Caherciveen. Once I got there, it was getting pretty late so I decided to treat myself to a night at a campground. I was hoping to work out a way of getting back to Portmagee without having to cycle. This the guy at the campground did with aplomb, booking my trip, getting me picked up by the skipper and all without commission.

That's something that has hit me about the Ring of Kerry people. Despite the fact that the area they live in is one of the most touristy in Ireland, they don't seem to be dominated by the tourist dollar. Maybe it's because I'm not travelling by the typical means but the people that I've met are happy to help me out, have a yarn, and give a wave, all for no charge. Feels like there is a strong community spirit here. One of the better photos I took back in Glengarriff was of a burnt out car dumped next to four different types of recycling bins. I thought of entitling it 'Waste Management'. However while I was having a beer in the pub, the locals turned the conversation to the car which had just been dumped the other day. They were adamant that a 'tourist' or 'tinker' did it because: "No-one in this community would do something like that!" That may be true but to me it highlights the insular quality of the Irish spirit.

 *Monks*

Got up early (for once) so that I could pack, have a break etc. before 9 a.m. As I hadn't previously timed myself, I was surprised that it only took me just over half an hour to fully pack from scratch. Not bad.

The trip to Skellig Michael was great. Little Skellig is a bird haven and as we approached, the number of birds circling the rock became apparent. At first they looked like bugs circling a light in the wetlands as there were so many of them and indistinct but as I got closer I could individualise the birds.

Michael however is the draw card and it is an amazing place. Pretty much it is a rock 15 kilometres out in the Atlantic with its only redeeming feature for habitation being its isolation. Monks colonised it in the 6th century and occupied it for the next 800 or so years. In that time they built some extremely hardy beehive huts and stairs that have survived almost untouched due to their impeccable construction – and the fact that no-one could steal the stones to make walls.

Very impressive. Crazy to my mind but impressive. Camped just shy of Glenbeigh.

➡ *Blowouts and Punctures*

Determined not to waste money for the next week as have blown my budget already. This was put to the test while crossing the Slieve Mish Mountains when I had my first puncture. Not just any old puncture either but a full rear tyre wall blowout. Cursing and stressing I spent half an hour trying various methods to glue a tyre wall into place without any success. In the end, I used the pannier repair kit and duct tape and I got the tyre going well enough for me to get to Tralee, although I didn't sit down for the next hour to keep the weight to a minimum. Once there, I was determined to get a top quality replacement, however as there was only one tyre option available, I ended up spending only $12.50 for a new tyre and tube.

This worked out fine as I put the new, skinnier tyre on the front and replaced the rear tyre. All good, so I headed off for Listowel. It was starting to get late and there wasn't much sunshine left so I spent the entire 27 kilometre haul between Tralee and Listowel looking for a camp spot. I couldn't find anything suitable and I was beginning to despair when just shy of Listowel, I found a perfect site. Unpacked and prepared for another 12 hour sleep.

 Plain Sailing

(Thanks for all the comments people. It's good to see people are reading this as otherwise I'd get slack and forget about it…)

I can't believe the luck I'm having with the weather. Apart from yesterday when there were rain clouds coming from Kerry (which never eventuated), I've had perfect weather for cycling. That and the fact that tourist season hasn't started yet means that I've had plain sailing along the way, even on roads that would usually be packed with vehicles during summer.

I might as well keep to the day format as that way I can relive and remember.

 Irish Breakfast Roll

Cruisy day. Was right next to Listowel so once I was up went into town and bought a breakfast roll.

For those not familiar with Irish cuisine, which includes national dishes such as cabbage and bacon, anything with potatoes or deep fried; the breakfast roll is a revelation. In short it contains anything that you might find in a full Irish breakfast but in a baguette. Possible ingredients include: black/white pudding, bacon, omelette, fried eggs, mushrooms, sausages, onions and whatever preferred sauce. It is different in each location and the contents can be a pleasant surprise. As a meal, it's always filling. For a country that abounds in deep-frying, stouts and carbohydrates, you'd expect the Irish to be a much fatter race. However apart from the main cities, there is a definite shortage of fast food outlets with the main 'convenience food' being in a SPAR or Centra, which are deli/convenience stores.

Anyway, after breakfast, I went to the Kerry Writers' Museum, which had a very artistically laid out display focused on five famous Kerry-born authors whom I'd never heard of.

I then headed north to Tarbert to catch a ferry into Co Clare. I managed to get a free ferry ride as I couldn't work out where to pay and when I disembarked, I queried this with the deckie but he just waved me on. I found a campsite in a wood just outside Kilrush and decided to go into town to watch the big soccer match.

Gaelic Sport

I thought it was the FA Cup Final right up until the end when Man U were defeated and the one Irish guy supporting them said, "Oh well, at least we can still win the cup." The pub was practically empty despite the soccer broadcast, and the afore mentioned bloke was the only one interested in the game. Co Clare is definitely GAA (Gaelic sports) territory.

When I showed my interest in the game, the bloke bought me a beer and I would have happily returned the favor but he turned out to be a full blooded red-neck. Whenever a black guy got the ball he cursed the 'dirty nigger' and went on and on about 'Russian mafia', 'no pride in Man U' etc. So I cradled my beer and once the game had finished I fled without a word.

Amazingly, the Irish think they live in a multicultural society. Amazing because hardly anyone isn't white. There are a few Africans, a tiny number of Indians and I can probably count on my fingers the Asians I've seen, usually working in food shops. The only feasible minority I've seen is the Eastern Europeans and mainly in the main cities.

Peat Man and Misunderstandings

Pleasant surprise, as the hidden wood that I thought was out of the way, was actually a large park that contained a restaurant. I was woken up by two ladies who said that they had had, "A beautiful breakfast at the restaurant and couldn't eat another bite." So they dropped off some scones replete with butter and jam. After breakfast in bed, I headed off for the Cliffs of Moher. Most of the cycle was uneventful except for the fact that I kept getting lost. Clare isn't as well marked as Kerry. I hugged the coast stopping to take a photo of an old pensioner and his pile of peat (compressed bog used as firewood and fertilizer). At first I thought it might be a bit inappropriate, asking him to pose for the photo, but he was more than happy. We then had a genial conversation full of misunderstanding.

I tried to explain that we didn't need firewood in Darwin as no-one had fireplaces (to his disbelief). He tried to explain some complex horticultural process involving peat which produces great potatoes. Eventually I remounted to a chorus of 'God bless' and continued on.

Finally found some damsels in distress. Two ladies had a flat tyre, so I asserted my manhood and changed their flat. After that good deed, I was on a bit of a cycling high, and raced some small bird (which I would have called a singing bluebird except it was brown) along the road. I kept up with it for a fair way until the slope steepened.

The cycling has definitely got easier as my body has begun to adapt. My legs feel good and my bottom and back only get sore if I have had too long a stint in the saddle. Even my bowel motions seem to have co-ordinated. As I rarely camp near a convenience, I only seem to feel the urge when I am presented with a nicely ordained tourist facility or service station. In all, I am quite impressed with my body so far. The Cliffs weren't as impressive as I expected though, especially after Skellig Michael so I headed off for the Burren to camp.

Burren

Cycled the Burren that looks a bit like an open cut mountain rock mine. I ended up taking a number of photos of old ruined churches and forts which abound here. Despite the fact that the land looked pretty infertile (rock plateaux) it was all partitioned by rock walls, a feature that is constant throughout rural Ireland.

I think that some of the rock walls were only built to maintain a consistent pattern as there seemed no reason to partition some of the areas. I especially got that impression in the Burren as the land looked unfarmable.

Powered through into Galway where I currently am. Put all my clothes except my Cork hurling top and shorts into a laundrette as my clothes were really starting to smell after a week and a half. Wearing a Cork top outside of Co Cork is kind of like wearing a Collingwood jumper in inner Melbourne. I wasn't too sure if it was a wise move, but so far I've had a few 'Up Rebels' calls and no-one has spat at me yet.

Went to the pool to find out that I could use it after 6 p.m. so I am going to have my first swim in seven months and my first shower in about a week. I'm almost giddy with excitement. Have to go as laundromat is about to close.

 Mayo Magic

Mayo has a bit of a bad reputation in fact, the Irish even have a saying which goes something along the lines of 'Mayo, God help us.' However, from what I have seen of Mayo, I have been more than impressed.

After my swim, launder, shower and Chinese takeaway (banquet for two) I was feeling quite clean, suave and sophisticated.

I headed off early to Rossaveal to catch a ferry to Aran Island and totally out of character, I got there early. Luckily because the ferry departed half an hour earlier than the Lonely Planet stated but it was all good and I managed to spend quality time with a huge group of loud, American college students. As I had taken a while to board (a bike with panniers isn't made for a gangway) I had warning so I got as far away as possible and the first question I was asked, I answered "Ne comprede."

Aran Island was a bit of a disappointment because it was supposed to be a 'must see' place and although it was stark and contained some very nice pre-Christian ruins, I was pretty much quarried out with stone buildings. That and I couldn't help comparing the Island to Skellig Michael, which in my book, was far more impressive. However there was some mountain bike riding on the back end of the island so I spent a quality day traversing those tracks.

One more thing, I definitely got a bad vibe from the place, hard to quantify but I was quite happy to be back on the mainland. It had been a really windy day and was getting late, so I headed north on the lookout for a campsite. The actual cycling was pretty brutal as the terrain was open and I was pounded by the wind. When I finally found a site, I was exhausted and didn't bother cooking, just ate some bread.

←→

The best day cycling I've had by far. Last night, the initial cycling was brutal but once I hit the Joyce Mountains, they provided a windbreak and I cycled through the most spectacular scenery. First the Joyce Mountains, then after Leanne there was another mountain pass along a lake that was stunning. The day itself was sunny and I even managed to get a bit burnt. I'd almost forgotten that the sun could do that.

A quality day all round as I had a really nice lunch in Leanne and found a pearler of a campsite on a beach in

Murrisk. Cooked a proper meal and considered going to the pub as there were a couple of big boxing matches on and the Heiniken Cup Final but was too tired so crashed after watching the sun set over the ocean – the first time I'd seen that since leaving Darwin.

I considered staying in the same site another night because it was so good – soft grass, a natural concave ridge on both sides and a stonewall meant that it was almost fully enclosed with the only open side looking across the beach. But in the end, restlessness prevailed.

 *Croagh Patrick Pilgrimage*

I packed and then headed off to Croagh Patrick, a big hill (almost 800 metres) which is a pilgrimage site as St Pat spent the forty days of Lent up there. That, and it's also the mystical place where he banished the venomous snakes from Ireland and sent them to Australia. I mean really, you don't have to be a genius to work out that if they are banished from one place then somewhere else is going to be stacked with a multitude of fanged slitherers.

The actual walk to the top was pretty steep. The view was spectacular, best so far by a mile. The bloke at the shop said that we were really lucky with the weather because quite often fog or clouds could interrupt the view but today was

another sunny day. I could trace my previous days' route through the mountains and was even able to work out a projected route for the next couple of days. The visibility was so clear that I could see plains after the hilly range to the north. Waltzed down the hill and passed a number of sorry pilgrims. I felt a bit sad for a few of them but I knew that they were probably earning penance through their suffering and they had a natural gift waiting for them at the summit.

Headed off for Westport where I am now. I'm off to watch a movie and relax tonight with something fast and fatty for dinner.

 Westport

I'm writing this on mate Geoff's computer and don't have Internet access. Hopefully there won't be any problems because the last time we tried to do this, my update was lost when Geoff updated his operating system.

My update had been full of gratuitous compliments to all the people I had worked with in Cork but I have a sneaky suspicion that it was 'lost' due to a number of sheep shagging references to all the Kiwis I had met in Ireland.

As I was still pretty sore and sunburnt from the cycling and hill climbing, I decided to have a day off and take it easy. Watched Kingdom of Heaven a hack and slash movie with some easily digestible religious and moral statements and found a decent pool complex. To my joy, I pretty much had the pool to myself, so I made the most of it and swam to my heart's content. The complex also had a steam room, sauna, spa, plunge pool and footbath and by the time I had used all of them, I felt totally clean. I even contemplated getting a massage but baulked at the price. I felt a little guilty because I have often bemoaned the fact that Ireland seems to be a swimless society with decent pools being impossible to find but since I've been on the road, I've found a couple.

Westport is a charming little town with a very nice layout and amenities. I spent the day wandering around until the weather started to get chilly, then I headed back to my tent and spent the rest of the day cooking, eating and reading.

Saw a couple of fully kitted out cycle tourers complete with entire ortlieb pannier set up. Their bikes looked like miniature cars and put my two small panniers to shame. However, I got a fair bit of satisfaction watching them manoeuvre their bikes around as they looked way too heavy to me.

 The Waving Game

After yesterday's break, I considered heading off for Achill Island but the journey would have added a hell of a lot of kilometres and all the information I had read indicated that it was a fairly rundown, peasant community and I've had my fill of those. Instead I decided to head for Sligo.

The cycling was fairly uneventful, but the roads weren't busy so I got the iPod out and started having a bit of a sing along and playing the waving game. The waving game involves trying to get someone in a 'rich' car to acknowledge your presence. As a general rule, people in beat up cars, tractors, trucks and old four wheel drives will give you a wave when you nod to them as they drive past. However, people in Beamers, Mercs, Audis, Toorak tractors or convertibles are much harder to get a response from. I'm not sure exactly why but I guess that the average 'rich' car owner weighs up the cost/benefit and decides that the energy required to give a wave exceeds any social networking benefit that the wave may generate. After all, a guy cycling by himself in the wilds of Ireland is hardly going to be an influential stockbroker. Over the course of the day, I managed to get a wave from one BMW and one flash looking Fiat. Not too bad considering that traffic was pretty light.

Once I hit Ballina though, I was condemned to travel on a major road, which was the curse of the next couple of days as there were few side roads going in the direction that I wanted.

Finally reached the Ox Mountains and found a great little camp spot at the top of a very steep hill with a wicked view over Sligo Bay. While climbing the hill, I managed to herd a couple of sheep up as well. I apologise to whoever the farmer is who has to round them back up but the stupid animals kept running up the main road and wouldn't take any of the side routes on offer.

Surefooted Sheep

Awesome descent this morning. Went for a fair few kilometres on the rocky back road and don't know how I didn't get a flat. Managed to scare a heap of quietly grazing sheep – note to self, don't buy any lamb in Sligo as meat bound to be heavily stressed and gamey due to maniacal cyclist ringing bell and braying at innocent lambs. Found out that sheep are quite surefooted and can run very fast down steep slopes. One thing for certain, I'm glad that I'm on a mountain bike as once you get off the main roads (and even sometimes on them) the roads are very dodgy and you wouldn't want to ride with anything less than thick tyres.

Sligo was fairly forgettable, lots of one-way streets and traffic jams. I went to the Yeats museum and the information on him was fairly good.

There was an art gallery as well, but it was without doubt the worst gallery I've been through. The artist on display was either 3-4 years old or specialized in kinder art as all the 'items' looked as if a preschooler had done them. If the prices weren't $300-400, I would have thought it was quaint. After the first room, I popped my head into the other rooms to make sure there wasn't anything different in there, unfortunately no.

Comments such as 'Exciting', 'Interesting' and 'Nice

frames' were in the guest book. I added 'Beyond my scope' as I really couldn't work out how such a big gallery could be filled with such rubbish.

The weather took a turn for the worse and the rain came, so I got to my projected campsite as quickly as possible and camped on Bullin Bay beach.

▶ Gallowglasses: Scottish Mercenaries

Nice easy day. Got into Donegal and had lunch, then headed off for Killybegs the fishing capital of Ireland. Took a photo of a tombstone with a gallowglass on it. Gallowglasses were Scottish mercenaries who fought in Ireland and I've always been fascinated by their name.

Mates Geoff and Cazz then drove in and we found accommodation in a really flash hostel, a room with an ensuite and a BATH. I ended up having two baths and a shower in my time there and the hostel was luxury. We got some fresh seafood, had scampi, smoked mackerel and salmon for dinner mmm. Despite Cazz being pretty tired, as she had done all the driving that day, we then went to the pub and had a good night out playing pool with some Portuguese fishermen. Nice bed, no tent, bath, seafood, beer and pool – seventh heaven. Ahhh.

Smoked Haddock & Bermuda Triangle for Irish Bachelors

After utilising the showering facilities one last time as well as getting a quick (three hours) launder, Geoff, Cazz and I had a fried brekkie of sausages, beans and eggs. That combined with last night's smoked mackerel and scampi meant I had plenty of propulsion during the day – and not just in the legs!

I went back to the seafood place and got some more smoked haddock and salmon and ended up having a chat with the old fisherman. He was a really nice bloke and he even gave me some cooking tips:

"Aye son, around these parts it can get pretty cold."

"No?"

"Yer, so what ye do is cook the smoked fish in some milk with whatever spices ye want in it. Sort of like a soup."

"How much milk?"

"Oh ye know, just enough to cover it."

I tried that and it worked really nicely. I didn't actually make a soup, more a fish-cooked-in-sauce and added it to rice and it was pretty damn tasty.

The fish seller also told me about a friend of his that had

gone to live in Darwin.

"Aye, he met a lassie and headed over there. Fifteen years and no-one has ever heard of him since."

I enquired after his name and description and verified that I had never seen him either. Enough information I think to cement Darwin as Australian Bermuda Triangle for bachelor Irishmen.

Fully provisioned up, I left Killybegs and headed north. I didn't really have much of a plan except to follow the coast. Donegal has a reputation of being a wild and beautiful coastline and I can verify that it is both. The riding was at times pretty hard due to the lack of level ground, wind and weird weather but some of the views were outstanding.

I found a little visitor centre in the middle of nowhere near Narin called the Dolmen Eco-Tourism Centre which was a 'green' building (lots of use of renewable energy). It had a very impressive archaeological and geological display but the attendant seemed a bit put out that he had a visitor. I don't think they see too many as no-one came while I was there and I almost felt like I was intruding on his goodwill. So in order to annoy him, I spent a decent amount of time viewing all the exhibits, then the toilet, then a coffee... I swear, the guy was almost ready to pull his hair out. After that little diversion, I headed off for the 'Rosses' a sort of summertime retreat, and set up camp next to an ancient stone circle across from Donegal Airport. The old, the new and the transient.

Snapped Spokes

Wow sun. Yesterday had been pretty gloomy but I woke up to sunshine. Did a check over the bike and found that two of the rear spokes had snapped. Remembered that yesterday I had heard a loud sound but had thought it was a stone rebounding off the frame. Two spokes, both on the interior side meant I would have to take the cartridge off to get to them!

Set off to find a bike shop to borrow tools. This proved a futile exercise as there didn't seem to be a bike shop anywhere. At the servo where I stopped, I was given a lead.

"Letterkenny, they'll definitely have a shop there, Oh, but they'll be closed by five (it being Saturday)."

Getting to Letterkenny by five meant that I would have to revise my route and head over the Derryveagh Mountains, which in a way wasn't too bad because the views were great. The weather however wasn't. It poured. Then it hailed. Wow. Water that gets so cold it actually freezes and it's like stones coming out of the sky. Unfortunately they weren't able to help me in Letterkenny, but they kindly gave me more spokes to fix the two additional spokes that had broken in the meantime. Set up camp outside Letterkenny and had the 'Smoked fish in the cold weather' as per instructions.

Belfast Bound and Slash Town

Checked and fixed the spokes I was able to reach without taking the cartridge off and then decided to set sail. I knew that I probably wouldn't be able to get any help until I got to Derry or Slash town as I had been pre-warned to call it.

'Slash' was due to the unfortunate naming situation in which the border town has found itself. Protestants call the town Londonderry, the Catholics call it Derry. Apparently the correct way to approach this situation is to call it Derryslashlondenderry but for those non Welsh people amongst us you can get away with calling the place Slash town.

Before I reached the Slash, I had one more appointment that I had to keep in Eire and that was to visit Muff. Muff is a tiny town north of Northern Ireland (as most of Donegal is, which is kind of strange), and many pubescent jokes had been made about the place once we'd found it on the map. As it was on the way, I couldn't disappoint Geoff by telling him that I hadn't seen Muff this cycle trip. I could make a few cracks about it, but I won't because my Mum reads this, however I will say that Muff was a bit disappointing.

As it had been ALL day, it was wet. In fact, today was the wettest day, so far, on the trip. I got absolutely drenched which isn't much fun over the full course of the day. My one ray of sunshine was that I found a shop with the right tool to take my cartridge off and I could finally get the spokes fixed. Promising my suffering bike that I'll be giving her a service soon, I soldiered on through the rain. (Yes, Stormbringer is female, and sometimes I talk to her.) Finding a campsite was a lot more problematic than normal as both the potential campsites that I had envisioned (picnic sites on the map) turned out to be nonexistent. In the end, exhausted, I camped next to a church. Well, it was Sunday. I promised myself that I'd have tomorrow off if the weather didn't improve as I had lots of food, and water didn't seem to be a problem.

$$\longleftrightarrow$$

Rain, rain, rain. In a sense I was quite happy to see all the weather so I didn't feel guilty about taking the day off and settling into a day of doing nothing. I had the Sunday papers, which were huge and good reading and I read through the first section to the last page – the weather. Sunday's weather, as experienced, was very wet. Today however the weather wasn't too bad, still that wasn't enough to convince me to change my plans. Tuesday's weather did though. Wet, windy and worse than Sunday. Groan… It was about 11.30 a.m. when the rain seemed to have stopped. I started packing. I had just got the tent done when the rain began again. This time it began to lash. Cursing, swearing and gesticulating, I finally managed to get everything packed half soaked. I headed off to the nearby town and took shelter in a telephone box. Thank God for reverse charges. Rang Mum and Dad in Australia and had a bit of a chat.

Luckily, the heavy rain stopped by the time I had finished the phone call to my parents and so I decided to head off with the goal of reaching a major town and staying in a backpackers so that I could dry everything out. I couldn't wear my sneakers as they were soaked. Yesterday my feet had gone totally numb by the end of the day and I wasn't willing to risk another full day of cold feet. Funnily enough, waterproof socks don't work when your sneakers are soaked. So cycling away in my glorified sandals and cutaway socks, I set off for Belfast.

As I passed through the interior of Northern Ireland, I noticed a marked change to the countryside. Firstly, the stone walls were disappearing, replaced by hedges (probably fueled by the abundant rain) and normal fences. More affluent buildings were on show and there was a huge decrease in the pubs. I crossed over the Sperrin Mountains and was greeted by a beautiful sight. Blue sky, ahhh. The rest of the day was a breeze and the weather improved and the traffic was a lot lighter than in Eire except for a short stretch when I had to cycle along the A6, which is a feeder road into a motorway.

Cycling through Antrim, I thought I was passing a big jail – 10 foot high fencing, barbed wire and more cameras than any major sporting event could house. It turned out to be an army barracks. Barbed wire was very scientifically placed in a number of locations.

I got into Belfast at around 2030 and it was dead. Shops were closed and it took me a while to find a bed at a backpackers, but on the third attempt I got one.

↔

Up early and spent the day cycling around. Went to the

Belfast botanical gardens, museum and City Hall. Booked my ticket to Scotland, the ferry to Stranraer for tomorrow to venture into the land of haggis, kilts and hairy people. I'm almost at the end of my Ireland sojourn. All I've got to show for it is a dirty bike, wet gear, photos and some great memories. I'm definitely going to miss Ireland. I've managed to survive seven months here. Not a bad achievement considering that after living in Darwin, I hadn't had a winter in over a decade. I've met some great people and the Murphy's and the craic have been great. Still, time to sail for (hopefully) sunnier horizons.

Went back to the backpackers and starting typing up blog when I met Big Kev who was on holiday with a Canadian mother and daughter. Big Kev seemed a bit worried to be in Belfast (him being a southerner and all) but we managed to get through the night without any problems. This may be partly due to the fact that we spent most of said night trying to find an open pub. We succeeded in the end and I had my last pint of stout on Irish soil.

Scotland: Gammon

Wet, windy and dreary. I got off the ferry at Stranraer and thought 'What next?'

Well, that was easily answered, I needed to find a map. Started cycling down a main road and found a service station. The maps there weren't to my liking, but I was able to work out that I was going in the wrong direction. I planned my route of attack – follow the coast. One thing I noticed was the huge selection of soft porn available in the service stations, which was never apparent in Ireland. Lots of porn but no decent maps, looks like titillation rules over direction. Headed north along the coast which could have been quite a nice cycle if the rain had stopped.

Bought some food in a small town and finally found out what jaffa cakes are like – quite nice. Later on, I stopped at a fish and chip shop to get some warmth; I was about to order haggis and chips when I saw 'gammon' on the menu. For those non Territorians gammon is a fairly common word which sort of means 'dodgy'.

"What's gammon?" I asked the chipper girl.

"Errr, I'm not sure."

"Is it any good?"

"Well, I don't eat it. It's kind of like a meat thing."

"Gammon chips please." (If I said that back in Darwin

the owner would probably query why I was calling his chips dodgy.)

"Err, it's deep fried," the chipper girl said.

"Gammon?" (Gammon can also be used as a query, it's a very versatile word.)

"Yes," she said eyeing me suspiciously. "In oil."

"No worries," I said, as she ran off probably to get away from the weird, wet, smiling Aussie.

Decided to pay for the night camping as I knew my tent was wet and I needed a shower. Set up the tent in a gale and then ran to a pub to watch the Champions League Final. Great match. I take back some of the stuff I've said about soccer. Ended up cooking dinner in the shower block, which wasn't so bad as I had a couple of hot showers and a hot dinner.

After yesterday's deluge, I woke up shocked to see the sun. Decided to make the most of it and set off straight away. Stopped in Ayr to buy a map to work out what to do and ended up buying The Hitchhikers Guide to the Galaxy Chronicles. I was really close to Glasgow but I didn't want to turn up at my relatives out of the blue so I thought, why not head north?

Headed further north along the coast to catch a ferry at Dunoon. Once again the scenery was great and it was awesome to be cycling in the sun again. Checked the paper that night and good weather was forecast for the next couple of days. Cool.

Rain, Rain, Rain

Left my tent once during the day for a water refill and nature call. Spent the day dozing, eating and reading.

My experiences so far in Scotland have been black and white. It has either been pouring with rain or sunny. On the fourth day, I worked out that of the 96 hours I have been here I have only had 9 hours without rain. That said, one constant has been the impressive scenery, easily the best so far; roads that have been well maintained and have sensible contouring have also helped with what has sometimes been a pretty hard slog.

↔

Rain, Rain, Stop. I woke up early (5 a.m.) and started packing for what in my mind would be the inevitable end to the rain. After all, the weather men couldn't be wrong two days in a row? After a couple of hours, I unpacked my sleeping bag and spent the rest of the morning reading until a break in the weather appeared. Like a flash (ok maybe a small spark), I had my tent and bike packed and was off.

However, the rain break was just that, a break. Once I was all packed the rain started again, almost gloating. "Ha ha, I got you out of your tent, you're mine now Dry Boy."

I got the ferry over to Dunoon and probably against

standard wisdom, headed further north. The scenery was beautiful but marred by the constant drizzle. I climbed over a mountain range and I swear I have never ridden through such wind/rain. It was pretty foggy and the cloud line was at the summit but still I had to pedal the whole way down the rise as the wind threatened to blow me back up the hill. I finally gave up once my feet went numb, which seemed to be my wet weather threshold. Found a camp spot and spent half the night warming my feet up.

Woke to grey skies, a bit of a cough and lowered spirits. Still, it wasn't raining and people had been talking about how the weather would turn good on Sunday. Today was Sunday but I had lost faith in weather predictions and was beginning to wonder if there was such a thing as good Scottish weather.

 # Welcome to the Highlands

My fears were unfounded as the weather did come good. Not good enough for me to take my leg warmers off but I only wore two layers (instead of four) and the sun shone all day. Awesome.

I headed off for Glencoe and was rewarded with the best day's cycling so far. I entered the highlands (there was a big sign that said: Welcome to the Highlands) and though I spent most of the day pedaling uphill, it was a nice enough gradient that felt quite comfortable. The scenery was spectacular as it slowly wound through the glacial valley. The only bad thing during the day was that I took a side turn to a ski resort (up a steep gradient), which promised Internet access but wasn't open. Spent a long day in the saddle and was rewarded by a lovely beach campsite just shy of Fort William: soft grass, Sunday papers and a bottle of wine although, after one glass I was asleep.

↔

Scotland has many wonders, natural, historic and man made. One of the best I have come across is the wonder of how anyone could live this far north during the wetter months?

↔

After yesterday's sunny reprieve, there could only be grey. Grey and the sound of lawnmowers. Yep, my grassy oasis recluse was about to be mown. Quickly packed up stuff and headed off for Fort William. Before I got there, I decided to have a swim in Loch Lochy (which I guess must translate as lake lakey) as I was feeling pretty manky.

Had breakfast in town, wrote up blog, shopped and then off. The weather kept getting worse and I was getting more and more annoyed with it. In the end, I gave up. I pulled up next to a phone box and spent the next hour reading Sunday's paper in there waiting for the rain to ease, The weather section said today would be sunny and then gradually digress until Thursday, which would be a shocker. Hmmm.

Once it had calmed down a bit, I went off in search of a campsite as I was a tired from yesterday's big cycle.

➡ *No Camping RIGHT*

On my RIGHT hand side along the Loch, there were lots of signs stating no camping, so I camped on the LEFT hand side. I wasn't too sure if I was bending any rules so I hid behind a clump of trees. No problems. In fact, despite never checking the camping policies of Ireland and Scotland, I hadn't had any problems with my campsite. No-one has ever told me to move on, which (touch wood) shall continue.

↔

Reluctantly, I opened the fly of my tent – to sunshine. Woohoo. Dried my kit and packed. Promised myself that a launder was due as everything was beginning to smell pretty rank. Headed off for an easy day's cycling along Loch Ness.

Stopped at Fort Augustus for a feed and managed to convince a young American kid that the Loch Ness monster only ate little boys, especially foreigners. Kid didn't want to go fishing with me and eyed the Loch with new dread. Well, he shouldn't be talking to strangers, should he?

I decided to take the back route around the Loch after I eyed all the tourist buses there. Most of my past near-death cycle experiences have been at the hands of bus drivers. For some reason unbeknown to me they seem to relish cutting the closest possible overtaking line to cyclists. Why? I don't know. There are lots of vehicles just as big as buses but they all seem to understand that you're giving them as much room as possible and they either slow down or give you a wide berth. Buses however, seem to want to take out the lone cyclist. Maybe it's because I haven't bought a ticket? Anyway, in order to avoid the lumbering death transports and their flocking cargo, I headed east when they went west.

It was a good decision as the route was quiet and very pleasant but it involved climbing easily the steepest hills I'd come across. Granny gear got used to its full potential and I had to make a few stops to… err… take in the view.

Ness was very scenic, but to me it just looked like a wide river and it's hard to believe that it contains more freshwater than the rest of the British lakes combined. It really got me thinking about how small Britain is. Got to Inverness and came across the North Sea route, the 6000 kilometre bike trail that I'll be more or less following from now on. To celebrate, I had an 'ultimate kebab and coke' – the party animal lives.

Battle of Culloden Dreams

Still light, so I headed for the Culloden battlefield (which was closed) but I found a decent wooded camp spot right across the road. The (alleged) start of summer is heralded in

Scotland by a grey wall of cloud and continuous drizzle.

I had a number of fairly depressing dreams last night although none of them really stood out. Went to Culloden and bought a Heritage Trust membership so that I would have some sites to aim for. Saw a map of the battlefield and realised that the Heritage Trust didn't actually own the whole battlefield and that I had camped on part of it – maybe where the McDonalds were slaughtered – I wonder if that had anything to do with my strange dreams?

After witnessing enough gory tributes, I picked up the bike route and came across some awesome cairns (old burial mounds). Really impressive but I can't remember their name.

Following the bike track was good fun despite the constant rain as there was hardly any traffic and I had hardly any brakes so we kept one another guessing. I reached Brodie Castle (Heritage Trust) but it was closing at 4 p.m. so I was

Culloden – the spirited dreams of old battlefields.

too late. The weather was supposed to be really bad tomorrow so I found a decent campsite near a tap and toilet expecting to be confined to the tent for the day.

↔

Woke early and the fly was dry. Poked my head out and saw that the sky was a lighter shade of grey. Spent a while agonising over the possibilities but in the end, I decided to make a dash for Elgin as I needed to do some bike maintenance, have a shower, launder etc… The weather held while I made my quick dash and I found a laundry to dump my dirty clothes, which included everything except my Speedos, sport shorts and hurling top.

"I'll have it done by five," the lady yelled.

"I might be frozen by five," I contemplated.

 *Juggling Tricks*

Next, I found a bike shop, bought some brake pads and ended up having a fair yarn with Billy the juggling, roller blading, 63 year old parking attendant. He got me a bucket and cloth so I could clean my bike and also let me use a car park for the next couple of hours while I gave her a service. A really nice guy, we ended up trading juggling tricks.

As my pale blue complexion was generating interesting looks from passersby, I headed for the swimming pool and spent the rest of the afternoon there (except for writing this up in the library) avoiding the elements.

Am about to pick up my laundered clothes. Luxury.

↔

It has rained continuously so my main cycling kit was wet today. I decided to take a chance and cycle in my groovy slippers instead of the cold waterlogged boots which I couldn't bring myself to put on. Turned out to be a masterstroke because even though the clouds were 'menacing' (defined later) the sky had pity on me and it never rained heavily enough for me to need to get my boots on. I also ended up going bush for a while which meant that my lovely clean bike is now all messy again.

Menacing – adjective, descriptive
1. intimidating.
2. Scottish weather when the clouds are constantly grey, the air constantly hangs with a pre-rain humidity smell, there is constantly a pre-rain breeze but it is not actually raining.

Yep, amazingly despite the clouds being menacing all morning, the water stopped for a while and I was gifted with a reasonably dry day. I headed west and brunched near Buckie at a bakery. I had a fair conversation with the lady there as she extolled the virtues of the 'brodies' (steak pies), 'softies' (soft plain buns), and some name that I can't remember (fruitcake). As I only went for the brodie and the fruitcake she ended up giving me the softie anyway ("Ye cannae com here and nae haa a softie"), plus the coffee for free.

Having freeloaded most of brunch, I followed the bike trail through the countryside and came across a joiner museum in a small town in the middle of nowhere. It wasn't well advertised, a small sign off the main drag, and I only noticed it because I was on a toilet lookout. Went in and it had a decent display of tools and memorabilia from the turn of last century. It would have been paradise for Mick (my chippie mate) and I enjoyed my time wandering through.

I got to Turriff and had to make a decision. I could stay on the bike route which would mean less traffic or I could choose my own way and visit some of the heritage castles that were in the area. I chose the latter and ended up at Fyvie pretty late at night.

Heritage Trust Buildings

The castle gardens at Fyvie were huge and as I had done a fair day's cycling, was pretty tired and hadn't seen any decent camp sites for a while, I marked time until it was dark and camped in a secluded spot in the castle grounds.

'After all,' I thought. 'I am a fully paid up Heritage Trust member.'

Saturday and I was woken by the sound of a helicopter landing in the castle grounds. As it was raining and the castle didn't open until twelve, I stayed in the tent right up until then, wondering who might have been in the helicopter:

S.A.S.? Royalty? and whether they might have spotted my tent from the air.

The helicopter turned out to be part of an Open Day display that Mobile/Exxon was having. 'Open Day' was a bit of a misnomer because it was a private party for Mobile employees. I was however, able to tour the castle and the tour unfortunately exited into the Mobile 'Closed Day'. As no-one was ushering me out, I watched the sheepdog and falconry display, had a chicken fajita, coffee, salad, hotdog, another chicken fajita and then was busted going for another salad. One of the attendants pointed out that I didn't have a Mobile sticker, unlike everyone else, and that this was a private party. Through a mixture of intense politeness, feigned ignorance and blundered apology, I headed to the official entrance where an official took over. I then re-explained my ignorance to more officials and offered to pay for my salad. They laughed and said it wasn't a problem but that I would never be allowed to badmouth Mobile/Exxon again. I swore that I would only use Mobile Service Stations to fill up my water bottles while I was on the road (unfortunately, I have had to renege on that one because I haven't seen any Mobile Service Stations).

It was by now too late to visit Haddo House so I headed for Inverurie as there were a number of stone circles and standing stones there. The Grampian region has been heavily (comparatively) populated for a long time so there are lots of castles, Pictish standing stones, stone circles and cairns scattered around. I won't bore you with the individual details but over the next couple of days I visited a number of each.

Damp Map Problems

Camped in a forest. Am a little bit lost, as my map which has been saturated for a number of days is falling to pieces and I am currently over one of the missing pieces.

Was heading for Craigevar Castle but due to afore mentioned mapping problem ended up at Drum Castle. Once again, that was the only one I could visit due to time restrictions so I decided that instead of waiting in the castle region, I would pick the bike route up again which I did at Stonehaven. There was an impressively huge castle/ruin there but I can't remember the name and it was closed so I spent most of the day cycling. I ended up camping next to the beach on the North Sea. At last, I properly feel like I'm on the North Sea route.

←→

Another day mainly filled with cycling. Highlights included getting freshly smoked haddock at Arboath – actually that was a big highlight so I'll expand on that. I was cycling along the harbour when I smelt the smoker which was pretty much set up in the guy's back yard. I went to choose a couple of fish inside the actual smoker and ended up eating them both on the spot mmm.

Cycled through Dundee which looked like a pretty nice

city except that everything was closed. Flirted with an Irish girl at a supermarket (one of the few places I actually contact people nowadays) and ended up at an awesome camp spot in the woods across the Tay.

Golf Epicentre St Andrews

Headed off track again for St Andrews because well, you have to go there. Heritage saint and all, golf epicentre of the world.

Golf is Scotland. There are golf courses everywhere and it seems that due to their lack of success in any team sport, golf rules. This, I agree with of course, and I only wish I had more time, energy and money (golf is pretty expensive here) and I would have a few bashes. On the way I passed an air base with a decent crowd waiting at the end of the runway (some with chairs). It looked like they had been there a while, so I thought they must be protesters.

No, they turned out to be plane nuts. As I had nothing better to do, I waited as well and was rewarded 15 minutes later by a couple of jets taking off. That provided about 15 seconds of entertainment and I wondered whether anything else was going to happen as no-one else was moving. Five minutes later decided that nope, nothing else was happening, so I moved on. I spent the next hour or so wondering why people would wait hours on end just to see planes take off and land, and eventually came to the conclusion that some people are pretty sad.

Unfortunately, time was not my friend again so I only got to go to one museum (the National Golf Museum of course) and despite pleading, the officials looked with disdain at my request for a bash at St Andrews. Booking, neatness, finance and etiquette being necessary for anyone wanting to play a round.

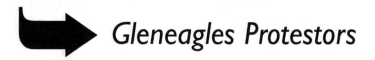 ## Gleneagles Protestors

It was getting dark by the time I found a campsite near Gleneagles chosen more through desperation than position as it was pretty close to suburbia, something I try to avoid. Later on, I realised that Gleneagles was where the G8 Summit was to be held and people were pretty worried about feral campers populating the area thanks to Bob Geldof's 'One million protesters' call. Luckily, I was only there for a short while and gone before anyone could make it an issue.

 *Relative Values*

Wow, it's been a fortnight since my last confession. Bad sign, but my laxity has been through laziness and not any major mishap. That said, the details about what has happened over the last couple of weeks will be a bit foggy…

I won't bother doing an executive intro but the past fortnight can be divided into two parts – cycling in Scotland and playstation in Newcastle.

I escaped Gleneagles without being caught by any protesters against the G8 Summit, locals, officials or dog walkers (the latter usually being constant visitors around my campsites), which was quite strange considering how close to the suburbs I had been. I picked up the cycle route straight away and was treated with a great single track following the Forth Harbor. The cycling was good fun but I had to remain mindful of not picking up too much speed as there were a lot of walkers and blind summits and corners. More than once I was thankful that I had brakes again.

I have to say, I love the names the Scots give to their rivers. It's as if someone with a speech impediment named the rivers by counting them as they headed north: Firth, Thecond, Tird, Forth…

After I headed forth across the bridge, the weather started to deteriorate so I hurried into Edinburgh and found a

backpackers to bunk down in. There, I met some Kiwis and one of them had clippers that I borrowed and took two months growth off from my chin and scalp. That combined with a very necessary shower meant I felt cleaner than at any other stage of this trip. We then went to watch the Lions beat some provincial NZ team and spent the rest of the night deriding the Lions and the rest of the English sporting nation.

$\longleftrightarrow$

Big day. Woke around 5 a.m. as a couple of people in the dorm noisily spent half an hour packing at that ungodly hour. Went and did an update on the blog and then decided that I might as well head to Glasgow as I didn't really want to stay at the backpackers and pay £12.50 for 4 hours sleep. I originally thought I would spend a couple of nights there because I was trying to work out how to meet up with Geoff and Caz again but the travel bug was itching and I wanted to get to Glasgow to meet my relatives. I packed my stuff and went to Edinburgh Castle. Flirted with the Aussie attendant at the castle but I couldn't wangle a discount so I spent a good 3-4 hours wandering around until I felt that I had justified the entrance fee. That said, the castle was spectacular and well worth it.

Sustrans Maps

I found that it was impossible to find any Sustrans maps (Sustrans stands for sustainable transport and they are the group that maintain the bike routes around the UK) of related areas. The maps that they make were very good quality (cartographically as well as their manufacture) but they were very narrow minded in that they only focused on a specific area. I would pay big money if I could find a good overview map or a collation atlas or book with all the bike trails marked. That and Sustrans' distribution was hopeless, as I couldn't even find the relevant maps at the start/end locations.

I was told by a person at the backpackers that the Union Canal ran all the way between Edinburgh and Glasgow which indeed proved to be the case. This has led to three days of very happy cycling as I had good sunny weather (mostly) and was able to cycle along a scenic, flat bike path. I put in some good yards (I'm picking up the imperial vernacular) and pulled up early so that I could camp before I got to the outskirts of Glasgow.

One big point of interest was the Falkirk Wheel which is a huge rotating boat lift. It was made so that the 11 traditional locks could be bypassed. I arrived at the wheel while it was in action and got talking to another cyclist (who gave me all the above information). The cyclist seemed like the canal equivalent of a train spotter and after a while I got a little bored.

"Dam, that's wheely impressive," I said trying to insert humour into the conversation

"Yes," he said unsure as to what I was doing.

"It's like a lock quay," I continued, chuffed at my on-the-spot witticism. "Boats barging through."

"Hmm yes."

The conversation died then as I couldn't think of any more analogies and the rotating lift spotter realised that he hadn't found a fellow enthusiast. He left and I spent the next couple of hours wondering whether I had bored a boat spotter and if that was the case, whereabouts did that leave me on the conversation chart? Pretty damn low I'm thinking.

Another thing worthy of mention was that during the day I came across two people who were in bad pain and I felt unable to help. The first was a kid who must have fallen and either dislocated his shoulder or picked up a fracture. The second was a pregnant lady in a parking lot who seemed to have gone into labour. In both the cases, a fair crowd was surrounding the suffering people, so I just left as there was nothing that I could add to the situation. Both times I pondered on the fact that medicine is such a great skill to have and apart from basic first aid, I cursed my lack of knowledge.

Sunburnt

Slept in today as I only had 10-15 kilometres to go until Glasgow. Yesterday I cycled without a top as most of the way had been reclusive and the sun was out. I am a little paranoid about how white my body is (not my arms and legs but under my shirt and shorts) as in this country of fake tans and UV machines it's kind of embarrassing to say that you're from a hot country but are incandescent when you take your top off. I surmised that if I took the opportunity to get a little sun during the gentle Scottish heatwave then I might even be able to get a tan when I am in Europe. So of course I managed to get burnt on my back, which is crazy considering that most of the day I was quite cold with my top off. The sunburn wasn't too bad though so I arrived in Glasgow in high spirits, found a campsite in the middle of nowhere, showered, shaved, and then went to meet my relatives.

Aunt Agnes, the Scottish Relative

It took me quite a while to find the house as the maps I had didn't cover the required area and the road that the guy at the tourist shop told me to follow, was the wrong one. Still after asking lots of people directions, twice as many as I needed to because I could only understand half of them, I finally found the right house. Despite not giving any warning about my impending visit , and never having met or communicated with them before, the relatives were very hospitable and genuinely pleased to meet me.

We worked out that Aunt Agnes was my mother's first cousin and she was a lovely lady. We had tea and cake and corrected misconceptions about each other's family.

↔

I got back to the campsite late that night very tired as I had done a lot of cycling around Glasgow. Slept in again, decided against staying at the caravan park for a second night (£10.50 for a dodgy tent site without toilet paper or soap) and headed back to Edinburgh. I was trying to work out how I could meet up with Geoff and Caz again but I wasn't sure when they were arriving and I didn't really want to hang around as I wanted to get to Newcastle to meet my mate

Mark. In the end I decided to cycle along the canal again as I knew it was a gentle ride. Found a campsite and then tried to find a pub so that I could watch the Lions/Maori game. Unfortunately, couldn't find one and gave up after about half an hour of searching.

Grand Scottish Weather and Headwinds

Typical dodgy Scottish weather. Today it was sunny and warm to begin with, then cloudy. By the time I got to Edinburgh suburbs, some freak cold front swept through and I got drenched. It was amazing. I swear the temperature dropped by ten degrees, the wind picked up by 20 kph and the rain just lashed down.

Soldiering on, I decided to visit the zoo as when I had been at the Backpackers I had seen that they were looking for some Australians for a koala display, hopefully as guides and not behind bars but the pamphlet didn't elaborate. Pondering this while cycling along the canal I decided that if the job was for around three months or so I would grab it. Might be fun and Edinburgh looked like a good city in which to spend time. Unfortunately, I found that the koalas had been delayed until August which was a pity because the contract was indeed for three months and would have worked out well.

Deciding not to stop in Edinburgh as I am a cheapskate

and didn't want to pay for accommodation, I headed to Newcastle. This proved to be a poor choice as over the next few days the weather went bad again. Kept cycling until pretty late at night when I found a nice campsite in a forest enclosure above a waterfall.

↔

Really, nothing sticks in my head about today. I remember I cursed a lot. It rained a lot. I ALMOST told a shop attendant to stick the weather where it doesn't shine after he smugly commented about "Grand Scottish weather," but held myself back on two counts. Firstly because it would have been a bit rude but mainly because as I surmised to myself, "The sun doesn't f------ shine anywhere in this b----- country."

The only place flat and dry enough to camp was underneath some large power lines that were bulldozed through a wood. Spent the night listening to them sizzle and spark as the rain hit. A bit disconcerting when you're camped so close.

↔

This write-up is occurring at 5 a.m. while I wait for a train so I doubt that my memory is going to be as efficient as it could be. By avoiding paying for a hostel, I'll finally be able to get this blog up to date, something that I've been meaning to do for a while. The main problem has been access to computers as I don't want to stop during the daytime when the best cycling is to be had.

What do I remember about today? The singular thing that sticks out most was the Newcastle headwind. A bit unfair really because I did a lot during the day – got well lost, passed a number of Northumberland castles, got drenched, cursed, cycled in my estimation around 100 miles from dawn (not quite as dawn is at 4.30 a.m.) till dusk. Despite all that, one thing cemented into my mind is the headwind I hit on the last 20 miles into Newcastle. Varying in intensity, usually getting stronger when I was pedaling uphill, the headwind changed direction almost with perfect accordance so that it was always blowing straight into me. The only time it stopped was when I would have a break and even then it would blow on cue to extinguish my zippo.

Newcastle Rest Week

Either English weather wanted to prove that it could compete with Scotland, or the Scots weather had loaned itself south for a couple of days to pay me back for leaving.

That said, at this stage of the day, I was as tired as I have been during this trip but determined to make Newcastle. I knew I could crash at Mark's place as I had been told that the weather was going to get worse and I wanted to avoid that. So the lure of beer, showers, rugby and warmth kept me going.

For that Newcastle week I indulged in Mark's hospitality. Shower, beer, playstation, playstation, sleep, food, playstation, beer, beer, sleep, playstation, food, shower, playstation, beer, food etc... Mark has been a good mate. My body was

exhausted and needed a couple of days off.

On my previous Newcastle visit to Mark just after I arrived in the UK, I'd walked Hadrian's Wall and my old e-mail about it was still on his computer. I read it as if I was reading about someone else, but I still agreed with the sentiments.

Memories of Hadrian's Wall

Newcastle is a pretty ugly town with lots of red brick and not much else. It looks like someone, at sometime worked out how to build a square brick house and then to save time (that could otherwise be wasted by thinking) everyone just copied the design and built lots of square brick houses. Every now and then someone did something risqué like render the bricks, or build a house out of stone, but they were obviously freaks. All right minded Geordies (Geordie is a person who grew up in Newcastle) built square brick houses.

Newcastle does have some bridges and Geordies are very proud of their bridges. I think they are so proud of their bridges because they have some steel in them, but I'm pretty sure that it would have been a struggle for the engineers to convince the Geordies not to build the bridges with bricks.

I found from the tourist information office that you could walk from the east coast to the west coast following Hadrian's Wall. For all those people that were truant when they should have been in History class, Hadrian's Wall is a wall built by Hadrian a long time ago (for more info check out the book: Big objects that can't be seen from space). The original 73 miles long Hadrian's Wall, was built in Roman times to keep the Caledonian 'Barbarians' from invading Roman controlled England. Most of Hadrian's Wall was destroyed when the English built a road on top of it — ahh you have to love the conservation movement.

Seeing as I haven't done any exercise in the last month due to an unfortunate injury, (injured self in Darwin by falling over the bike handles) I went out and bought a tent, some supplies and decided to take advantage of the small window of sunshine that was available. The walk was very nice although there weren't many campsites on the route with most people staying in hotels along the walk. Being too tight to stay in a hotel, I ended up camping illegally on farms when it got dark. Luckily, I was never caught so I don't have any amusing stories about farmers chasing me around paddocks firing buckshot etc... I did however have a few testy moments with some sheep and cattle, and was bitten by a Scottish terrier that came very close to Doggie Hell but for the most part the walk was fairly uneventful.

A word of warning to anyone planning to walk the wall — the first couple of days there is hardly any wall left along the walk. The third day though is awesome as a bloke actually bought up the surrounding farms in order to protect the wall and there are these long stretches of undulating craggy hinterland with a big wall and lots of remains of

Roman forts. I was also very impressed with Carlisle Castle, which is a big stone castle.

At one of the museums along the way, I bought the book The Ninth Legion, which is set in Roman times around the wall region. After I had bought the book, the museum guide told me that it is required reading in English schools for 9 to 10 years old so it was stretching my literary standards a little. Luckily, there weren't too many big words in it and it was a good read. In all, the walk was very well maintained and serviced and I have seen enough ruins to see me through winter.

At the moment, I'm back in Newcastle and I found a group of computers hiding away at the local library. To all the people who have written to me, thanks for the encouragement and I'll try and get back to you soon.

Until then, I'll leave you with an ancient Geordie blessing: 'May all your walls be made of red brick.'

↔

Then I found the second old e-mail. Again like reading of another person's life.

 *Walk it*

Mark and I went to watch the soccer match at the local pub. That's two soccer games I've watched in the last four days in what must be a record for me. From what I've seen, the English aren't very good at soccer. I mean their sporting facilities are hopeless and they don't have much in the way of organised coaching networks. I went for a swim the other day in what looked like a new swimming pool. The pool was all of 20 metres long, had no lane ropes and trying to do laps in it was like playing dodgem cars. After I'd done a frustrating set of laps, I had a chat with the pool attendant.

"So, are there any full size pools around here?"

"Ooo ai."

"Yeah? Whereabouts?"

"Why here!"

"No, no, I mean, are there any Big Pools?"

Blank look.

"Olympic size. You know 50 metre length."

Big smile.

"Orr, no. We don't have any of those in Newcastle."

Well, if that was the situation, then I'd have to live with it. I thought that I'd better get in early to get a decent swim, so I checked the opening times expecting them to be

around 5-6 a.m.

No.

Monday – Closed.

Tuesday – 9 a.m.

No wonder they can't produce Olympic swimmers.

Anyway, I've got a bit off topic. I went to the pub last night with great expectations as I had been reading the complete bagging that the press had been giving the national soccer team after its 2-all draw with Austria. One of the papers even had a donkey saving the equalising goal that the unfortunate English keeper had missed.

So there I was at the pub, barracking for Poland. Unfortunately, England won, although for a while it looked like Poland could pull off an unlikely draw. They may not be good at it but the English take their soccer pretty seriously.

A bit dejected after the win, Mark and I went to have a game of pool. I ended up playing a Geordie, a very serious bloke, who strutted a bit and said lots of things I couldn't understand. He beat me in a close game but then Mark beat him in the next game. The Geordie walked over and said, "Walk it."

I didn't have a clue what he meant. I thought, 'Maybe he wants us to go outside and have a blue just because he lost a game of pool.' But no. 'Walk it' as a young girl later explained to me is local slang for "No worries mate, you're all right and we don't have to fight unless you really want to." The girl then explained to me that I needed to support an English soccer team as otherwise I would be thought socially inept. Then I would be allowed to badmouth the English team all I wanted, but I wasn't supposed to cheer when the opposition scored a goal. Thanks to this new education, I now support Middlesbrough United because they have a couple of Aussies and a bloke called JimmieJimmieJimmie and I think that David Beckham is a useless sod who couldn't kick a round ball through a square net.

Walk it Trev.

↔

The weather had turned good and my body felt good, the bike had been cleaned, so south I headed. The plan was to get to York to try and catch up with James. Route undecided because even though I had a week to plan ahead, playstation and reading old e-mails had occupied my time.

Route Markers Vandalised

Once I crossed the Tyne, I decided to find the No.1 route (North Sea route) which turned out to be a lot harder than expected. Sustrans routes are great in the countryside where most of the signs are intact but in and around the cities the routes are practically impossible to follow due to vandals defacing, destroying and turning route markers around the wrong way. I've lost count of the times I've tried to follow a route and then given up in disgust after countless wrong turns or missed marks. In the end I just ploughed along horse trails and rights of way in the generic direction of the sea until I hit South Shields and picked the trail up. I then followed it along the coast until I lost it again in Sundarland, picked it up again, lost it in Seaham. This time however I met a couple of girls touring with a map so we managed to get properly lost until we fluked the route through trial and lots of error.

I had a brush with death at Peterlee. A lady driver pulled out in front as I was flying down a hill. I don't know how she didn't see me, it was a steep hill so I was keeping pace with a car in front of me and keeping to the middle of the road as I wasn't delaying traffic. I guess she didn't think I was doing the speed I was, as she pulled out after the car in front of me. I hit the brakes hard straight away and that was just enough to save me. I was too shocked to swear properly at her before she raced away ostentatiously checking her rearview mirror. Re-living it now, I still can't believe that she pulled out in front of me like that.

After that highlight, I kept going but my energy was running low after a long day so I started to search for a campsite. I couldn't spot anything before Hartlepool but found a spot in the industrial area before Middlesborough.

➤*Transporter Cycle Scene*

Crossed the river Tees on a Transporter, which is kind of like an automated ferry as it transports a pontoon across the river. According to the bloke I chatted with while waiting for it to get to us, it's one of only a couple in the world. Quite an engineering feat, lots of steel, pillions and cables but I couldn't understand why they didn't build a bridge as the River Tees is very fordable at the crossing point.

"It's just them hanging onto the old ways," the bloke told me.

I nodded sagely but thought, 'What old ways? Isn't a bridge older than a transporter? Why build something that has all the support, cables, reinforcement etc. but only uses one pontoon and staff to run it?'

Lost the route in Middlesborough but serendipitously while trying to find it, came across an Australian pub. Went in for a beer and found the cricket was on, so ended up having lunch and wasting some time there. I also found there was a route that went directly to York which I presumed would go through the Moors so I decided to follow that. Ended up camping on the outskirts of the Moors near a reservoir and had a swim before crashing.

25% Gradients

Cycled through the Moors, or more to the point, practically skirted around the Moors as the route circulated between small towns. The going was very hilly with the gradients recorded which was cool because I now know what a 25 per cent gradient is like (very, very steep). The towns and roads in the Moors were recovering from a flash flood a few days previously which was still pretty evident with a number of bridges being washed out and quite a few large bins filled with personal belongings that had been ruined.

Roads were pretty muddy too, so my nice clean bike was now all muddy again.

Did some shopping in Thirsk and then found a campsite in the back lanes.

That'll have to do for now as I'm pretty tired.

Catching up on a French Keyboard

Well, I'm a long way behind on my updates I'll be brief to catch up. Am writing this in France. This French keyboard, like everything else in this country has a strange setup – AZERTY instead of QWERTY. Ok, today I finally catch up... 2 weeks en rapido.

$$\longleftrightarrow$$

Looking back, I cycled the rest of the way into York; on the way picked some strawberries from the roadside that had a real honesty box. No lock and all £10 on show. Left my money. Got into York in the afternoon and went to find a pub to watch the first Test . Found out it wasn't showing until 9 p.m. so decided to find a campsite. Saw a heap of tents (seriously, hundreds of them) on the racecourse so I snuck in and pitched my tent.

Went into town to watch the All Blacks thrash the Lions – I was the only person in the pub interested in the match and they kindly changed one of the small TVs onto Sky Sport for me.

Found out that I had snuck into a bicycle rally meet and for once I didn't look out of place. Still, I felt a bit gammon for sneaking in, so I left early. Went for a swim and shower and my morning coffee but was a bit peckish so thought 'Stuff it' and bought a full English (breakfast that is). It was still pretty early and I was the only customer so I had a yarn with the chef. After I finished brekkie he made me up a latte, his specialty. Score.

Had a look around York Cathedral and the Treasury House then headed off along the cycle trail. Everyone else from the rally seemed to be on the same trail, so it was pretty busy but after a while the crowds thinned out. The rest of the day was a hard slog through ugly coal reactors. I remember losing the trail on a number of occasions and doing some trail blazing. One pretty harrowing part, I needed to get across a river and I followed a bridle way (English right of way over private property) I ended up slogging through a heap of farmland, throwing the bike over fences, along a tin bridge, more fences, a rail crossing and when I finally thought I was clear, I ran into an electrical fence – made of barbed wire to rub it in. I got through, but only through sheer bloody mindlessness.

Got to Doncaster which was a hole and looked pretty dodgy so I kept going, even though it was getting late. Picked up a trail the Trans Perrene Trail (which I followed for the next few days) and finally using my torch I found a campsite by a river.

Trans Perrene Trail and How NOT To Camp Illegally in UK

Followed the TPT all day. Pretty warm. I noticed how after a couple of days of warm weather, all the locals had their tops off and were either pink or lobster red that looked really painful.

Not too many memories, did some long yards, camped illegally (out of sight though) again in a National Park. I mean, where else do the authorities expect you to camp?

My only company was some sheep and I am thinking about writing a book about how to camp illegally in the UK.

Following the TPT again. Found out that I had a flat and broken spoke so when I reached a big town south of Manchester I called into a bike store got the bike fixed, did some washing, and went to weasel a shower from the swimming pool. The days are starting to blur a bit but I'm pretty sure that I kept trying to follow the trail even though it was almost impossible due to vandals. It got late and I couldn't find a campsite. All of a sudden, a heavy thunderstorm hit. I took shelter under a motorway overpass and as the rain kept going, I decided to cook some dinner while I waited it out. While I was cooking I noticed that there were some hidden

access routes to the core of the overpass so I camped there for the night in what turned out to be a great campsite.

 # Across the Mersey; Without Tuppence

Reached Liverpool and crossed the Mersey which didn't even cost me Tuppence; weird how some places have songs better known than they are. Reached Chester and headed along the north coast. There was a magnificent castle at Conway, really spectacular. That's all I can remember except that it was quite a pretty coastline with some great mountains shadowing it, and masses of caravans and demountables that populate the north Welsh coast.

Camped shy of Bangor just after a prepubescent kid ambled up to me and said in his toughest homie accent:

"You're scared of me aren't you guv?"

I went into shock and couldn't reply before he moseyed off, probably to cap some other niggers.

I mean seriously, I'm 187 cm, fit, tanned, smelly and a bit manic after a few days heavy riding. Why the hell would an eleven year old want to hassle me? I mean there were only two of them, and his mate looked scared just being there. Anyway, after I stopped laughing, I set up camp and puzzled over the kid for a while.

←→

Rush day to make the ferry. I didn't know what time it left so that only added to the urgency. Crossed onto Anglesey and didn't bother following the trail just picked up the A road (As are major roads). True to form Wales didn't want to leave me without some real weather, so it rained. I reached HolyIsland to find out that I had just missed the ferry. No worries, I caught the evening one and spent the rest of the day practising my juggling.

←→

July, wow, halfway through the year already. Whatever tax the Australian government lynched off me last year will all be owed back to me once I get a claim through. Talking about tax, that was why I had to go back to Ireland to find out what had happened to my missing Irish tax return...

Got to Dublin late... Too late for the trains or buses. The old hostel where I had once stayed wanted to charge me 20 euros for the night so I decided to follow the Grand Canal to see if I could find something campable.

Unfortunately, I ran into a group of knackers (tinkers or travellers to be PC) so I abandoned that theory. Seeing as there were only seven or so hours until the trains started running, I decided to buy a paper and slowly read it in a park. Made it until 0430 before I got bored and headed back into town.

←→

Spent four days in Cork catching up with old friends, having a few drinks and getting extremely frustrated with Ireland's service industry (or lack of).

 # *Irish Bureaucracy*

The tax office had sent me a cheque despite me giving them my bank details, checking off the pay-into-account box and double checking with an attendant whether that would be a problem as I wouldn't be able to receive any mail (he had assured me it wouldn't). My housemates had moved out, said that the mail was on the fridge. I went with the landlord but no mail. In order to get another cheque issued I had to get a waiver mailed to Australia so that I could sign it and mail it back…

I couldn't access my account from overseas (anywhere other than Ireland) by card, mail, phone or Internet to transfer money. The only way to do that would have been with a Cirrus card or credit card; both had been refused to me due to my employment status. There was a charge for closing an account so I kept it open and transferred all the money out of it. The teller lady looked a bit skeptical so I told her I was waiting on a cheque from the tax department.

Then the case of my missing backpack. The post office told me that the only way I could put a trace on the registered backpack (full of all my backup gear) that I had mailed to a friend for safe keeping was to have a receipt. I told her I had lost it as it was two and a half months ago but I could give a good description of it, along with the mailing date and location (there 80-odd days ago). The lady couldn't help smiling at my futile efforts, which really wasn't a good reaction to a: Yes-you-paid-$30-for-us-to-lose-hundreds-of-dollars-of-your-stuff-and-there's-nothing-you-can-do-about-it situation.

By then I was sick of dealing with Irish bureaucracies. At least catching up with friends in Cork had been good fun.

Booked a ferry from Rosslare as the ferry from Cork was $60 more and didn't leave until Saturday. I didn't want to impose on friends any more. Roscoff was 200 kilometres away and I had until tomorrow arvo to get there. Hit the road running (kind of). Decided to keep to the main highway as any other way was way too convuluted. I did the first 50 kilometres in a blur and then started to ease up.

Just after Dungarvan there was a big detour sign with flashing lights and a sign saying Rosslare This Way. Dutifully I followed the detour and ended up in Cahir before the direction turned east again. I later learnt that the detour sign had been set up to ease traffic for the big ship show in Waterford and that I needn't have worried about it.

This didn't impress me too much as it had added 40-50 kilometres to my trip but the policeman was quite helpful and sent me off again – in the wrong direction. Quite amazing really, I met three traffic cops in the vicinity of Waterford ('for the tall ships program, oh you shouldn't have worried about the detour sign'), each of them refuted the previous one's directions and only the last one put me in the right general direction. Camped outside Waterford cursing the Irish government.

Back on the main road to Rosslare until I finally hit a bike track and ran over something that blew out my rear tyre.

Fixed it and then scored a free coffee from a service station manager and got given a questionnaire to fill in about my trip in Ireland. As I had plenty of time to spare, I filled it in very comprehensively butchering the service system of Ireland – banks, post offices, garbage collection, road planners etc... but singing the praises of the Irish people. After all they are really genuine people. Spent the rest of the day practising my juggling and working out that I had left my general route guide at Kate's place! %#@#!

'Vous Anglais?' #shock# "Non, je suis Australian."

France here we are. Arrived in Rosscoff about eleven, fully prepared as always, my first stop was to get a map. I learnt early on that the French don't like to be asked, "Parlez vous Anglais?" as it invariably produced a deep sigh so my main tactic was to struggle along with my butchered French until they give up and butt in with their reasonable English. I also realised early on that everyone thought that I was English. Argghgh my worse nightmare has come true. I now talk (both French or English) with an extremely ocker accent and recently people have been mistaking me for Dutch or German which is definitely more agreeable.

From memory, I knew that the No.6 route (Nantes to

Istanbul) started from Nantes so I headed south. Bought food at the bakery – France is one big delicatessen, practically every shop specialises which means the quality is great, the prices reasonable (cheap compared to Ireland) but it can take four shops to get a baguette (bread roll), fromage (cheese), pommes (apples) et ou /eau (water) which has been my staple lunchtime feast. The bakeries and butchers are awesome though.

Camped in a wood on top of a hill and for the first time in ages could cook, eat and read outside the tent as no midges, rain or mosquitos, yeeha!

 ## Canal Bike Route

Kept heading south until I serendipitously found the Brest/Nantes Canal. This was a godsend because the route I had been blazing had been pretty hilly, the French drivers are as crazy as the Irish and I still needed time to accustom myself to continental road rules. The canal had a gravel bike route along its whole length, except at large dams and reservoirs, was flat and filled with the prettiest little 'lock' houses. I don't know what they are really called but they were houses set next to groups of locks, some derelict but a lot restored and beautified with flowers and bright, continental paint.

Followed the canal. I got into a routine of brunch in a lit-

tle village and then buying what I needed for dinner – down to two meals a day but both of them very hefty. The weather was quite warm, hot even and I had a problem finding drinking water as there were no taps on the route and I don't like carrying more than 2 litres on the back due to the weight and wine I invariably carried for, errr, cooking purposes ($1 for a bottle hmmm). I used the canal for cooking and bathing water but I once spent two hours criss-crossing a town to find someone open to buy water from.

Opening hours can be a problem in France, everything shuts between 12 and 2 or 2.30, the hottest and thirstiest hours, and Saturday and Sunday can be a lucky dip.

←→

Got to Nantes with my gear cable a mess after I had played around with it. Had a real love/hate relationship with Nantes. A very hot day and the tourist office didn't believe in being obvious. I searched everywhere but couldn't find a bike shop, tourist office, laundromat or even a local map.

Eventually, I found a bus station and they gave me a map with the tourist office highlighted. The tourist office was very helpful and gave me a free map which showed the completed stages along the projected No.6 route, about one fifth of the total route (the whole route was supposed to be completed that year). They also pointed out a bike shop, laundry and Internet shop on the map. I dutifully followed their instructions but wasted half an hour searching for the bike shop, all I could see was a Peugeot shop and another half an hour looking for the laundry which was non existent. I went back to the tourist office and the bloke looked non plussed when I told him that I could only see a Peugeot shop.

"Bicycle, velo, not motorbike," I said pointing at my bike shorts, gloves, map that he had given me and bike that was outside the glass window. Finally the penny dropped and he pointed me to another shop which was now closed for siesta. Luckily there was a laundry and Internet shop nearby so once everything was open I got everything done at once.

I had to trail blaze again as the route didn't start until Ancenis and I got a little lost and ended up on an island in the river Loire. I should have known that I was going in the wrong direction as the road ended and then became a network of single tracks surrounded by bush but I was hoping that it would clear up. I then went under a motorway bridge and I'm pretty sure that I stumbled on the gay meeting centre for Nantes. Everyone that I saw was male 20-40, walking solo with purpose, no fishing gear and would make eye contact and then ignore me. No "Bonjour" or "allo" which pretty much everyone else would do. After a while I worked out that the way I had come in was the only way out and I skedaddled.

Camped in a farmer's field feeling a bit like a trespasser but was well hidden. Picked up the bike trail at Ancenis and followed (what there was of it) until Orleans. I missed my canal as it was flat with no cars, full of cyclists (hundreds of cyclists) and camping spots. Now the roads grew steeper and even though there were still cyclists there were cars too, including the hated black-Audi drivers whom I have decided are the most obnoxious car drivers on the earth beating both Ford transit drivers and boy racers. Some cars go past too fast, some too close but only black-Audi drivers do both with annoying regularity.

Found a decent camp spot after following a single track

for a couple of kilometres and then was treated to a firework display. I couldn't work out what it was for until I realised it was Bastille Day.

Bastille Day in France

July 14th, Bastille Day. Marked by people honking their horns incessantly which can be a bit disturbing when you're on a bike. Did some fair mileage today and at Saumur passed a very impressive chateau that wasn't open. Can't remember much else except there were some visually impressive houses cut into the rocks along the way, and that it's impossible to find an open shop on Bastille Day. So my dinner was a very sedate affair of pasta, tomato paste and tabasco sauce. That and I found a great campsite on the river Loire.

Unfortunately, a spider bit me which was pretty painful but seeing as I'm fairly sure they don't have any deadly spiders in France and the fang marks were pretty small, I didn't worry about it. Fireworks again tonight with each town trying to outdo the other. As they were so close, I could see and hear the fireworks from three different towns as they took it in turns with the crowds cheering after each finished.

↔

Woke, had another wash, and headed off along the route. Did some reasonable mileage and got to Tours. Here, I went shopping for a small radio as the iPod is pretty useless because I can't charge it. The route stopped, so I blazed my way to Amboise where Chateau du Clos Luce is and, as everyone knows, is where Leonardo da Vinci spent his last years (umm, it was in the Lonely Planet guide). Paid the $12 entry – they're bleeding da Vinci code fever – but it was worth it because apart from the rooms in the dungeons and gardens there were models and working replicas of many of da Vinci's inventions; he really was a remarkable man.

Following the map that I had got from the Amboise tourist office, I saw that there was a trail called GR3 that was going in the right general direction. I decided to follow it but it turned out to be a walking trail, it wasn't sign posted and the scale of map that I had made it impossible to follow accurately. Still I found a reasonable campsite, (unfortunately not near a river) and used my drinking water for cooking. The forest was crawling with spiders and bugs and my patience was worn pretty thin, so war was declared and death to any insect in the tent. I got woken up during the night by something crashing through the bush. I didn't have my fly on and my night vision was clear but I couldn't spot any movement. I spent half an hour listening until I decided it must be a pig or horse and went back to sleep.

 Busking Bonanza

Tried to follow the GR3 trail but lost it almost straight away. I gave up because I realised that I had snapped a spoke that I needed to get fixed. Passed the Chateau Chaumont which was nice but I couldn't spot a good camera shot so didn't bother stopping. Got to Blois, had a look around, did my customary hour of aimless wandering, which is part and parcel with every French town I've visited, before I found a bike store where I finally bought a chain whip as I'm sick of finding bike stores to borrow one. Now that I have one, Murphey's Law dictates that my spokes will not break which is a fair trade. After having a look around Blois I realised how tired I was, so I decided to have an early night. Crossed a campsite almost straight away and seeing as I haven't had a shower in France yet decided 'Why not?' Camping was only $8, a lot cheaper than I expected.

I worked out that I was really dehydrated as my pee was a very dark colour so I spent the night drinking water and juggling. Unbeknown to me, as I had the walkman plugged in and my back to the road, some people must have thought that I was busking because when I finally turned around after a couple of hours there was a heap of coins (amounting to about $3). I know that I didn't drop them because my wallet was in the tent and I was wearing shorts with no pockets.

↔

Woke fully rehydrated (decent pee color) and tossed up whether to visit Chambord Chateau or not as I wasn't too sure how to pick up the track. As I was leaving the campground there was a large group on a bike tour, talking very loudly in English so I just presumed they were Americans, and they were being guided down some back roads. I followed until I had my bearings, and then overtook them. Visited the chateau and then headed to Orleans. I had originally intended to go to Chateau de Avery as well but somehow missed the bridge and then couldn't be bothered backtracking.

For lunch as per my policy of experimenting, I ended up with some really tough pork jerky style sausage. Absolutely gorgeous although very expensive. Found a really impressive cathedral at St Andre Clery with the remains of William the 11th and the heart of Charles the 8th in it. A noted classic of the flamboyant Gothic era the info sign outside stated and it was very impressive. I thought it was closed though after I had circled the building and saw all the big wooden doors locked. However I saw two more tourists enter through a door cunningly hidden on the side to deter heathens like me, though that trick will never work again.

Got to Orleans where everyone seems to speak English, or all the Moroccans I dealt with anyway. Without noticing at all I somehow got a wasp in my shirt and it chose to wait until I entered the Internet shop before biting me in the armpit. Ouch... My war on invertebrates continues!

Loire and Beyond

I've really got into the cycling routine and the fact that I haven't seen many Internet cafés or they have been horrendously expensive, has meant that I'm way behind again. Oh well, I can rectify that now...

The short story: Have been cycling through France, Switzerland and Germany to get to my current location – Munich. The long story is as follows:

After escaping Old Orleans, I cycled around for a bit, got lost, used my compass for the first practical time as I couldn't see the sun and finally found a campsite in a riverbed. While I was having a wash, a thunderstorm moved in and I had a brief panic attack that a flash flood was going to wash me away. That didn't eventuate.

↔

Kept following the river Loire although now it started to head south which wasn't really the direction I wanted to be heading. I stopped at a small tourist office in Chatillion-s-Loire, much to the surprise of the receptionist who I don't think received many customers in a day. She was more than helpful but of course couldn't help me find where the bicycle track was SUPPOSED to be – one of the best kept secrets in France. Camped just north of Cosne-Cours.

←→

Kept heading south until I hit the town of Nevers where I put past experience to use and headed straight for the train station in order to find the tourist office. This turned out to be a masterstroke because despite incorrectly marking the tourist office on the town map (I didn't have the heart to tell the lady that it was already printed incorrectly on the map) the office itself was contained within a labyrinth of medieval streets and the signs would have been more hindrance than help. After getting the customary free regional map with the customary 5 kilometres of bike trails into and out of the city, I visited the Gothic Cathedral. This was the start of a lot more visits to cathedrals as some of them are absolutely spectacular and they are free. I was so taken by the photos of the reconstruction work that I even donated 2 which from me, is like getting blood out of a stone. Leaving Nevers, I followed a canal that followed the Loire until I found a decent camp spot.

←→

Finally abandoned the Loire at Decize after making the decision to head for Switzerland. Stopped for lunch at Crecy and had a blowout on the main road to Luzy. I must have had a puncture a few days before because I didn't have a spare on me, so I had to repair the puncture and keep going. That was the start of a bit of a bad trend as I seemed to get punctures now with annoying frequency, probably every 3 or 4 days. I think the reason might have been that my tyres were starting to wear thin. I put in a fair day's cycling and my projected camp spot on a lake near Montceau turned into a bit of an

anticlimax as I couldn't find a decent place. In the end I camped next to the road hidden by a large tree.

N78 Red Cross Means?

Today was an experience. Not only did I cover a heap of kilometres, I now believe without a shred of doubt that the French are the worst drivers in the world.

I have had my fair share of drivers of various nationalities zooming past at high speeds seemingly oblivious to me but the N78 was something else entirely. I got run off the road by two truck drivers whose overtaking technique was akin to the Maori sidestep. Then had a couple of instances when I looked up and there was a car careening towards me in my lane because they couldn't wait 5 seconds till they got past me before overtaking. I don't care how settled you get with traffic, it's really scary to look up at a car playing chicken with you.

The N78, to its credit, had life-size cutouts of people on the side of the road with a big red cross through them. I don't know if they were previous chicken winners or reminders to the drivers that you're not actually supposed to hit people when you are in a car. If they were reminders it seems a bit strange to me because you really don't want people to have licences if they don't know that basic fact.

Apart from the death zone with its morbid tally markers,

I spent most of the day on back streets with the main obstacle being the growing hills now that the Juras (mountain range north of the Alps) were approaching.

↔

The trailblazing that I did was great because it was nice countryside with lots of vineyards. I even came across a long distance bike path but unfortunately it was going north south – Spain to Holland. As the day progressed, I decided to make a beeline for the Lac de Vouglans. I had already decided to have the next day off as I was pretty tired and I knew I was going to cross the Juras very shortly. That decision brought me to the N78 and my detestation of French driving for the rest of my life.

Managed to find an awesome campsite on the lake, hidden, next to a running river (with very drinkable water) so I spent the day doing nothing except drink, bike maintenance, eat (until I ran out of fuel so dinner was a lukewarm broth with uncooked vegetables mmmm).

↔

To cross the Juras, I knew I had to start on major roads so I made an early start. The first part of the day pretty much involved slowly climbing up hills with the occasional descent in between. There was a lot of traffic and I was getting a bit sick of the amount of diesel and petrol that I had to inhale… Sweet alpine air, yeah right.

 ## Swiss Time

I crossed the Swiss border at St Cergue and picked up a less major road and then had one of the best descents I've ever had. With the weight of the bike, it was almost like riding a motorbike when you've got long cornering descents.

Hardly any traffic and a great view over Lac Leman which is really stunning. The water is emerald blue, the French Alps are one side and the Juras are the other. I was sad when the descent ended because it had been so much fun.

I got some money out at a teller machine and the lowest denomination it had was a 200 franc note. A Swiss franc is worth a little more than an Australian dollar so right about then I decided that luxuries would be a no no in Switzerland. At Lac Leman, I decided against going to Geneva as it would have meant backtracking. I followed the Lake looking for a campsite which didn't look too probable, as there were houses everywhere. Eventually, I saw some tents in a field so I went and joined them.

It would be easy to go on about what I loved about Switzerland. The scenery is spectacular. There are water fountains everywhere with cold alpine water (no dehydration risk here). The country is organised, almost the antithesis of France. Within a couple of hours of being in Switzerland, I had a map showing me 9 different national routes and a booklet showing me the various cycle, walking and rollerblading routes available (unfortunately in French). The maps were pretty large scale and would have been useless for navigation but they were all that I needed as the routes were so well signposted.

The Swiss themselves seem an active people and were on the routes en-mass. Only when I got to the north-western areas did I get a bit jaded with the Germanic style: aloofness and tendency to stare but more on that later. Cycling along Lac Leman (have I mentioned how pretty it was?) I got to Lausanne to do my much needed wash and visited the Art de Brut Museum which houses the main collection of art generated by strange minds, something I could associate with.

I then headed to Montreux but it was packed with tourists and when another ferry load arrived I didn't bother going in. By now I had planned my route which mainly consisted of 'Route Panorama Alpin' and 'Route des Lacs'. First leg was up the steepest hill so far from Aigle, which according to the church bells I spent 2 hours in granny gear and still hadn't made the top. I did however find a great campsite and would have had a great sunset view over the Lake but clouds came and spoiled any possible photo.

$$\longleftrightarrow$$

I forgot to mention that yesterday when I was doing my launder, I saw an impressive piece of Swiss pride. A lady was washing her clothes and after she had finished her wash she took out the powder attachment, washed that, and then wiped the whole machine. I mean for someone to make sure that the machine was spotless for the next user was totally at odds with anything else I'd seen in Europe. It wouldn't hap-

pen back home either.

Anyway, I started the day near the top of a mountain and spent all day cycling up and down (some awesome down bits!) through ski resorts and alpine lakes. It was wet and windy all day but the rain was pretty haphazard and every now and then the sun came out. Near the Lac de l'Hongrin, I saw a couple of WW2 tanks that were there for some unknown reason. I thought that Switzerland had been neutral for the last couple of centuries. One thing though, despite their neutrality there were hundreds of discreet concrete entrances into the mountains that the locals say are arms and munitions dumps. There is even supposed to be a complete emergency hospital encased in a mountain somewhere.

The Swiss have to do military service and like the Yanks have very liberal gun laws. That combined with their knife making capability means that they are a country best left alone.

I came into a rich alpine valley containing the Chateau dÓex. The reason that I know that it was rich was because the village shops that had previously been bakers and butchers were now filled with Gucci and ski-ing equipment and people were walking around dressed in clothes that looked highly impractical and expensive at the same time. Even the bike shops were now high class with shops only stocking top range bikes and equipment (Cannondale and Rocky Mountain).

Despite the encompassing affluence, I still managed to spend minimal money with my diet of bread, cheese, chocolate, vegetables and pasta but I felt like a bit of a tramp when I pulled up to a cemetery and made lunch. Found a glorious campsite along La Sarine (the river). Glorious because it fulfilled all my criteria – discreet, close to water, flat, seats or tables and also there hadn't been any likely spots prior and I was beginning to worry.

Woke up and decided to brave the frozen river (I didn't have the courage last night) for what was the fastest wash I've ever had in my life – in, out, soap, in, out brrrr... dry. Feeling very refreshed, I continued to follow the glacial valley along some beautiful country. Most of the trail was dirt and steeply undulating which meant I got to play around a lot. When I finally got to the end of the valley (near Wimmis) it looked like they had sliced through the mountains to make a gap just big enough to fit a railway, river, road and bike path through.

I was now on the lake bike path and it took me to Interlaken a picturesque town between two gorgeous lakes – ThunerSee and BrienzerSee. To the south of Interlaken is a mountain range with a heap of 4000 metres-plus peaks and to the north are more mountains with which I was soon to become very acquainted. In short, the scenery was spectacular and I took heaps of photos – of mountains, waterfalls, bikes skewered on sticks (painted yellow, red and green for some reason), mountains, waterfalls etc. In amidst this Kodak frenzy, I had a coffee and spent the next couple of days thinking the lady had shortchanged me until I worked out that the 50 cent piece is the same size as our 5 cent piece back home.

I stopped for a drink in Miringen a bit worried as I couldn't spot a campsite. An old bloke started talking to me and giving me directions. He told me that I had to go up through a mountain pass that was encased by forest. I headed off in that way and it turned out to be the bike route anyway and still nowhere to camp. I pushed over the Brunig pass and eventually found a spot at LungenSee where I camped exhausted.

↔

My left knee was pretty sore today. It had been playing up since the Juras and was starting to get annoying. I had a great downhill run to ease into the cycling though and spent practically the whole day following lakes and watching the Swiss sun themselves on what turned out to be a glorious day. Unfortunately I wasn't able to spot any topless bathing which I had been assured by the Irish was everywhere in continental Europe. Ended the day on a mountain bike path in Untergerri.

Behind in Write Ups and Crash

Ok, so I'm an age behind on the write ups. Looks like I'm going to have to rush through to catch up.

Went to Einsiedeln Cathedral with the many clothed Black Madonna (they change her clothes each month). Had my first real crash along Stezlpass on some gravel when I was mentally miles away. Nothing serious, if anything a wakeup call to concentrate more when off-road. Patched up the grazes and got a great descent to Zurich See. Found a great camp spot along a river that had an artificial waterfall that was just like a shower, well the closest I'd been to one in a long time.

↔

Fairly sedate cycling, weather started to turn bad, unfortunately it was a harbinger for what was to come. Went through the Appenzell region, an enlightened place that only gave women the vote a few years back when a supreme court ruling labeled the men's conduct unconstitutional. Still, they vote by a show of hands so I suppose might only count male hands... Apart from politics, Appenzell had lots of brightly painted window shutters and people who liked to stare. I started feeling a bit self conscious and then pissed off at all the people who would just stare, but took no notice of any friendly greeting I offered.

In the end I found out that this was a fairly common Germanic trait and grew oblivious to it but at the time I was about ready to pull faces at people. Camped near some military storage site.

↔

Headed to St Gallen where an Irish monk founded a hermitage after falling into a blackberry bush and deciding that it was a divine sign. Irish logic at its best, to me getting caught in a bush is nature's way of detaining you for a short time, not a long one. Still the cathedral (yet another – more to come) was once again very impressive. The Swiss (and Germans) love gold trimmings, painted domes and 3D paintings (sculptures coming out of paintings). Going to cathedrals was like going to free museums. I had plenty of time. I wasn't meeting my parents until the 10th in Munich,

I decided to go around Lake Constance in an anti-clockwise direction. Crossed the German border at Konstanz and got a kebab... Ahhh it's been too long since my last authentic Turkish kebab.

 ## Disaster Day

Disaster day. I blew a tyre wall and destroyed the new tube I had put in yesterday. Seeing as it was Sunday, I managed to beg\buy a tube from a French tourer. Spent the rest of the day (after avoiding the tourist crush at a little island) with no front brake gingerly cycling around the lake. Found a great campsite with a sunset view over the lake.

←→

Well, that'll have to do 'cos I've spent a frustrating 3 hours with VISA across time zones between Australia and here, trying to arrange money transfers, and prove I am myself, and it's starting to get dark so I need to find a place to stay tonight. Without a functioning credit card, you're stuffed unless you can find a bank open when you are in a town. Luckily my parents are arranging an international transfer to cover the money that should have been paid in from the rent on my Darwin flat.

Munich Madness

The start of the German tour...

Limping into Friedrichshafen, I got a new wheel and spares, had a launder and was back on the road again. I went to the Zepplin Museum and for the first time in my life hired an audio tour as all the signs were in German. The tour was very detailed and in the end I just skipped through it as much as possible. Wandering through the displays you could be forgiven for wondering why the 'lighter than air' ships went out of mass production because there was only minimal reference to the 'disaster of ZV 10 something' and definitely no pictures of the explosion. I put this down to German airbrushing of history or a bit of blind eyeing and wrongly presumed that this would be the case everywhere. Continued following the lake until I picked up the Argen river and headed inland.

Followed the river by mainly blazing a trail which was quite fun because even the woodland paths in Germany are well maintained and most of the time in better condition than major dirt roads back home. I got to Wangen and at the tourist office was given a wonderful free map that showed all the bike tour routes through Bavaria. Awesome, I was spoiled for choice.

Following the Bodensee-Königssee radweg (bike path) I passed a large roadside carving with transport symbols strewn

all over it. After some deliberation, I decided that it must be the patron saint of transport so I left a small donation for luck – small because I'm not religious enough to believe it will make a difference but superstitious enough not to. As it panned out, the weather stayed lousy whenever I was cycling in Germany but I didn't have any accidents so fair's fair. Camped just shy of Immenstadt.

$\longleftrightarrow$

Lousy weather all day. I was interested in cycling up Jungholz which is this steep aberration in the German/Austrian border but the weather was so bad and cloudy that I gave it a miss. I'll always wonder what was on top of that hill. Slogged on avoiding diehard Nordic walkers and other mad tourers. Nordic walking is the latest fitness fad in Germany so I guess it'll only be a matter of time before intense Lycra and sweatband clad power walkers clutter the pavements with their stupid skiing sticks. I mean, ok if you're out bush then a walking stick, two even, is fine but on a flat pavement?

Wet and cold, I got to Fussen and was on the lookout for an early campsite. Had a couple of small lakes along the bike path pinned as definite possibilities but unfortunately those lakes were the backdrop for Neuschwanstein and Hohenschwangau Castles and their accompanying tourist hordes made camping impossible. Drenched and with numb feet, I cursed the castles and ploughed through the tourists using the Asian cycling technique – no brakes, plenty of bell.

In the end it took me a couple of hours to find a camp by a river but before reaching that I passed a really pretty water feature in the middle of nowhere. It was surrounded by a grove of trees, contained seats and was a water pond feature that you'd expect in a suburban garden not in the middle of a grazing paddock. Needless to say I was quite taken by the place.

←→

I was now on the Romantische Strasse which meant that I passed churches... lots of them, with lots of religious and historic significance. Unfortunately for me their main significance was a place to stop, have a rest and admire the frescos and paintings. Probably the best one was at St Weis but it was a bit disconcerting to see the numbers of tourists there. The weather got slightly better from the previous day so I piled some miles on. I knew I was going to get into Munich too early but I was ready for a decent break so I pushed harder.

I followed the Ammer river all the way into the Ammersee by (illegally) going along the water services access track for miles. Found a great sunset camp spot. Got busted in the morning by the water services ranger while I was having my morning wash in the lake. He started lecturing me in German and seeing as I was nude and couldn't understand a word he was saying, I just nodded and kept gesticulating that I was about to leave. Cycled along the Ammersee and then into Munich.

It took me ages to find out where the campsites were as there was a long queue of people at the Munich tourist office booking accommodation. It amazes me that the people who are most dramatic about having to wait in a queue will then proceed to occupy the attendant for half an hour. I was pissed off with the lady who had rushed to squeeze in front of me in the queue, spent the next 45 minutes silently complaining and then wasted 30 minutes of my time by occupying the attendant for that long.

My query: "Where are the campsites?"

Attendant's response: "Here, here and here (marking them on the map)."

"Danke."

Elapsed time – 45 seconds.

Camped at '*Tent City*' which is the major Munich campsite and had my first hot shower since the campground on the Loire. Fantastic.

All Things Munchen

Not a great day. I was crook during the night which I put down to food poisoning although I later found out that 'Kein Trinkwater' which was a sign at many of the fountains that I had frequented actually meant 'not drinkwater' instead of 'clean drinkwater' as I had presumed, so that might have had something to do with it.

Despite the day being overcast and myself being off colour, I was determined to go to the Deutsches Museum which has historic bike and clock exhibits so I rode into town. I felt worse as the day progressed and only spent a couple of hours at the museum before I decided to head back to the tent. However my bike had a flat and I had unloaded all my spares kit. Crook and tired as I was I couldn't be bothered working out a solution (catching bus/train or getting a patch kit) so I ended up walking the bike the 2 hour journey back before zonking out for the rest of the day.

I had learnt my lesson from yesterday so I did nothing all day and just relaxed and gave the bike a service. A pity because as it was Sunday the museums (apart from the Deutsches as we later found out) are free entry. Spent the day reading and sleeping and had one serve of milk rice for dinner because that was about all I could stomach.

 *Dachau*

Was feeling a bit better today so I decided to go to Dachau. Found my own trail through a maze of bike paths and roads which unlike the rest of Germany wasn't that well sign posted. As I was about to enter the main gates of Dachau, I suddenly got emotional and had to walk down a path to compose myself. Whether it was because of how run-down I was or all the confronting history that I have grown up with since I went to a Jewish school, although my family is not Jewish, but the entire time I was in Dachau, I had a lump in my throat and was on the verge of tears.

Loud American tourists breezed through.

"Look this one (cell) has got a toilet," voiced one as they brushed past me. I had just been reading the story of the prisoner who had been kept in the SS compound cell for 3 years and had been horribly tortured and couldn't believe that surrounded by such encompassing pain, suffering and fear the only thing the tourist could notice was the toilet facilities.

Later on, as I walked along the main drag, the only remnants were the foundations of the building and the trees that had been planted when the camp had just been built. In my guide book, the same trees were in some of the photos and were only slightly smaller. I resolved to take a photo down the promenade once I had got to the end to highlight the one living link still remaining in the camp. Walking to the end I had to listen to another loud Yank prattle on incessantly about some trivial, unrelated topic. I overtook them as quickly as I could and then fronted the promenade to take the photo.

The Yank then dragged her friend to get out of the photo claiming that:

"I don't want to be in his photo. I really can't understand how people can take photos of such a terrible place!"

"And I don't want you in this photo either but I can't avoid it," I growled back to the shocked woman.

Looking back, I really was exhausted and at the end of my tether but I wasn't going to have my motives questioned by a prattling Yank who couldn't divorce herself from her own self absorption for a couple of hours while she was in this 'terrible place'.

↔

Back at the tent I had a couple of showers as I felt very dirty. Didn't do much today. I think I was worn out from yesterday. I went into town for a bit and got some English books to read. My appetite was finally coming back so I ate a fair bit to catch up on the previous days.

Meeting my Parents

Today I spent my time cleaning myself up and packing because I was going to meet my parents. I couldn't download the itinerary that Mum had sent me because the attachment had a virus so I didn't know what time they were coming. I had tried to call them over the previous few days but couldn't get through. Mum had said that they were getting into Munich "very late" so I decided to hang around the railway station that night checking out the inbound trains from Berlin.

Unfortunately our interpretations of "very late" differed by 6 hours so I missed them. After midnight I gave up waiting (it wasn't the 10th anymore) and decided to check out the hotels near the railway station as they had said that they were staying right next to the hotel. I tried about 15 hotels to no avail then sent out an SOS e-mail to my sister Kim in Melbourne to see if she knew where they were.

Mum or Kim,

Is there anyway you could e-mail me where Mum and Dad are staying in Munich...

I can't download the file (I've tried on three different computers) that Mum sent me with their itinerary because it has a virus on it.

I can't seem to call Mum because everytime I try (5 times at 2.50 euros) it just goes to the answering machine.

I know that they're near the railway station but I've tried 20 hotels so far with no joy.

I'll check my e-mail every couple of hours or so as there isn't much else I can do.

Cheers

Trev

After sending that, I gave Kim a call and she directed me to the hotel that was literally 20 metres from where I was calling. That had been the second hotel that I had tried, but obviously they don't disclose who stays at the hotel, especially to shabby cyclists. Finally caught up with my parents at 2.00 or so in the morning. All relieved to see each other and Dad insisted on booking me a room and a big breakfast...

Munich train station, where Trevelyan searched for his parents.

Parents' Perspective Email

Dear Kim,

After a big message mixup and train time change, Trevelyan arrived at our Munich City hotel room at 2 a.m. SO VERY pleased to see him and he looks terrifically fit with big leg muscles. He checked 20 hotels to find us.

Your 1 a.m. call came through to our hotel phone and the phone was defective and just kept ringing. I couldn't get an answer, went to the hotel lobby but they would not permit outside calls, tried to ring you from railway phone outside just as phone card place shut. Lost lots of Euros. Tried on our useless phone card and couldn't get through even though lobby clerk tried. Then Trev knocked on door. We'd both been trying from the same railway phone box, at different times!

We talked until 4 a.m. and Dad booked him and the bike into hotel and we've had a short sleep and big breakfast. Thanks for being the link. So hard when mobile and other phones don't work.

We're looking forward to spending a few days together and feeding up Trevelyan.

↔

Spent the day catching up with my parents. We went for a wander around Munich, saw the Marienplatz, Englisher gardens and various other sights. I had stayed at their hotel that night but even though they wanted to 'shout' me the accommodation all week, I decided to keep camping at the Tent City, ten minutes ride away, after all it was six or more times cheaper and a campsite was luxury enough for me. But I did have baths in their hotel room. Hot baths! Lots of them.

We spent the day at Schloss Blutenburg an international youth library situated in a castle. Mum had set up an author visit there as sometimes I think that Mum needs every experience to be in some way workable in order to justify it. However the actual library was very impressive and we got a VIP tour of the site due to Mum's notoriety which was very nice. Some of her books are in the children's peace collection.

The only blemish was that I must have got disorientated when we were catching a train back and wanted to get the train going in the opposite direction. The spatial skills that have got me through Europe only seem to operate on two wheels it seems. Dad took us out to dinner, which I think became a bit of a fattening up exercise because Mum was worried that I was looking a bit gaunt.

Today was spent on a bus tour around a few of Ludwig the Second's 'fairytale castles'. Despite my reservations about tour buses due to continual attempts to maim me, it was good to sit in comfort and drive through the countryside that I had been cycling through. It was also good to get a second take at Neuschwanstein as my previous visit had been too brief and at a bad time. The bus tour also showed us some frescos which I was a bit ho-hum about as that was what I'd been looking at since leaving France. We went to

Oberammergau, the town which holds the 'Passion Play' every ten years, something that I'd never heard about before which marks a lack in my classical and religious knowledge. We wandered through the dramatic displays, but it wasn't a performance year. Dinner was my choice at 'Wienerwald' which I thought was going to be a sausage style restaurant but turned out to be Viennese style chicken parlour – Wiener is Vienna as Munchen is Munich and Donua (plus various Eastern European incarnations) is Danube.

Mum and I went to the Deutsches Museum as I really wanted to have a look at the clock and bicycle displays which I had missed earlier. Early bikes looked more uncomfortable than mine. Also found an historic maps exhibit which got me thinking. Luckily the bi-lingual captions were in German and English. Different methods of cartography had been used from hand sketching on parchment or paper, lithography, engraving on glass, scribing on plastic and electrical digital representation.

The exhibit info explained:

A cartographer draws a picture of the landscape as a bird's eye view. The task of the cartographer is to represent the curved surface of the earth on a flat map.

"You should know about that," said Mum.

I hadn't thought about the craft in quite that way before.

"I've been using maps, (or losing myself off them) not making one," I joked. "Lots of uphill as well as flat surfaces, so I have time to think about all the detours too."

"Your blog is a kind of mind map," Mum pointed to the exhibition definition, which she jotted down.

Carta = letter or original document.

Graphein = means to scratch or to draw.

That's the problem about having an author for a parent. They make you look for symbols and significance in ordinary stuff.

↔

During our Munich days together, Mum kept reminding me to keep the blog up to date or I'd lose some of my impressions. But I think Mum was just worried about me travelling alone so much and thought the blog was a way of expressing my emotions. I told her I talked to the bike too!

↔

As a family, we had a final late lunch together before seeing Mum fly back to Melbourne. It was great to have seen her again as it had been a year since the last time and I hadn't seen much of her over the past decade as I'd been working in the Territory. I went back to the tent to catch up on sleep lost since being at the campground due to noisy neighbours and access to artificial light.

Last day with Dad. We did the Third Reich Walking Tour with a tourist guide who was very informative. I never realised that Munich was the base of the Nazi party. Dad has always been keen on history and when I was little, we travelled as a family in Europe for five months, and we used to walk places like Waterloo and he'd explain what happened and why. We had lunch at the Hofbrauhaus which was the famous beer hall used by Hitler and his cronies and passionately disagreed about English sensibilities: Dad with his expat view of things English and my lager lout and English backpacker experiences. Intended heading off in the afternoon but after such a long break I wasn't looking forward to slogging in the rain. Instead, I stayed another night at the tent while Dad was about to leave for the Wagner Music Festival in the German town of Bayreuth where he would listen to the Ring Cycle for a week.

Nibelungenleid fountain. Related to Wagner's Ring Cycle.

 *Danube Donua*

Packed early, but then hung around the campsite waiting for the rain to stop. Got a little lost leaving Munich but was going in the right direction when I met an American on a bike who hailed me and we had a bit of a yarn. It turned out that he had cycled through America (west to east) and was

planning to cycle through Africa. He had stayed in Munich (18 years), due to having a child, but it was, "Only a temporary stop between trips." We were heading in the same direction so he directed me to the Englischer Garten (English Gardens) and I headed from there on my radar… All that mucking about trying to circumnavigate the town when I could have just gone into the centre and cycled through the gardens…

Uneventful afternoon, just cycling along the Isar river through nice wooded country. Camped along the river fairly early and cooked dinner to the excitement of various dogs being walked along the path.

↔

Weather unchanged. Was still cycling along Isar when I got a puncture on my rear wheel. Enough was enough. I had had so many punctures on the rear and I was pretty sure it was because the tyre had worn too thin. Fortunately I arrived at the next town (Dingolfing) just before the shops closed. I got replacement tubes and a new tyre and with no regret binned the old tyre and tubes. With a lot more confidence in my equipment (which was well placed as I didn't get another puncture until an unavoidable one in Hungary) I headed off and camped along the Isar again. Washing in the river was hard to get used to again after hot showers but I was pretty filthy after multiple tube and tyre replacements.

↔

Weather started getting better (slightly). Took a shortcut along the Vilstalradweg before hitting the Danube but it turned into pretty hard yakka as I battled continual headwinds along flat floodplains... Not much joy. Spotted a really cute church hidden in the woods but I think that was the only time the camera was unsheathed that day. Finally made it to the Danube and camped shy of Passau.

$$\longleftrightarrow$$

Austria bound... First stop Passau which I'm not too sure if it's Austrian or German but it's a very pretty city with lots of river frontage, impressive tunnels and walls and a living old town. By that I mean not just a touristy one but an old town where commerce and residence still exist. Kodak poisoning got the better of me and one day I'll work out why there were so many mermaids (sculptures) everywhere.

Cycling was a breeze... flat, well roaded and the accompanying headwind I'd grown to accept as my lot. Even toyed with the idea of cycling back to Munich to see if that would change the wind.

Cycle Tourers and Crash

Apart from the headwind, the other hazard was the number of cycle tourers. Entire families, and in one case a dog who was mounted in a crate on a well modified tricycle, were biking along the route at a leisurely pace. This mass of pedal powered lycra was at its most dense around Passau and then thinned out to nothing, the further east I went.

There were ferries everywhere to transport the cyclist across the Danube from one trail to another but I eschewed them, partly through stinginess and partly because the dirt tracks the ferries enabled you to avoid were in better condition than many of the tracks I'd followed.

There was one exception to prove the rule when I whizzed past a ferry station to be confronted with a wild single track that gradually grew into a walking track. There had been many signs that I had also whizzed past and in hindsight I think 'Rad… verbotem' probably should be respected in future. Walking my bike along the steep wooded path I eventually came along a treacherous gully crossing. I debated whether to unload the bike before crossing (which I didn't) and even took a photo of the crossing before attempting it. Five minutes later, I took another photo of the bike which had fallen 20 metres down the steep gully and I had some nice scars down my back. Luckily, my billy and stove which had come loose and fallen a further 50-odd metres came to a rest just before the steepest part of the gully. Otherwise they would have been lost to the Danube. After that heartstopper, I decided to get out of the gorge and took whatever upwards path I could find until I came to a road and then picked up the river again.

Was a lot more discreet in my campsite choice than usual as I had been forewarned that free camping was illegal in Austria.

↔

Next time I was presented with a ferry crossing I took it. Cycled past an array of sights… (they tend to blur) churches, industrial towns (Linz), villages, Viking boats. I stopped at a small bar and had some excellent wurst and an awesome wheat (wier) beer. Camped just past Linz.

↔

Sunday today and I had forgotten to stock up. Western Europe can be a real hassle to get supplies on a Sunday. I couldn't find an open shop and I didn't want to go into the touristy bar I found. Eventually, I went into a village restaurant but we had some real communication problems. I think it was along the lines of: I wanted to see the menu and they thought I wanted to order 'menu' which was off the menu. 'Menu' is generally an order which has a base entree, main and drink. In the end I gave up and cooked the last of my pasta for lunch. I eventually found an open store and restocked and by then it was getting late. Despite it getting dark and potential campsites being bare, I couldn't resist buying a beer from a vending machine in a small village. Underage drinking? How could that be a problem in Austria?

Camp location was a problem though because the gorge meant that there was no flat place to hide from the road. I eventually found a spot on the bank opposite a small town although I was a bit paranoid about getting busted.

↔

Bit of a blurry day. Can't remember much. Can't even remember campsite except that it was about 60 kilometres from Vienna.

Vienna Greeting Card to Family

Hit the gas today and got to Vienna in good time. Found the tourist terminal which actually worked in English unlike others I've found. Could even send greeting cards from it so I sent some to Mum and my sister to assure them that I was alive. Spent the rest of the day cycling around beautiful Vienna and its parks with classical music references everywhere. I had no intention of staying the night as the prices were astronomical. As always, Internet cafés were extremely elusive but I found one just as I was about to leave.

I quickly checked visa restrictions for the Eastern European countries that I was planning to visit. All turned out to be good except for Turkey which required one.

It was by now dark and I got a little lost before finding the Danube again. Luckily, the path out of town was straight, smooth and wide because I could barely see where I was going. I accidentally managed to trespass into some river port facility which turned into a boon when I found some bush to camp in.

Next morning left my camp quickly passing some confused workers who must have been wondering where I had come from (my camp was at a dead end). I found an outdoor cafe and stopped for coffee (a daily ritual). I had a yarn with some of the customers and the owner told me that I had to try Wienesse sausage so he cooked me up a plate of sausages... Awesome.

After that breakfast I headed for the border. I stopped in a town just near the border (can't remember the name but it was an extremely well fortified place with the old walls and hill fort very prominent). I tried to make a few phone calls with my credit card which was an option from Austrian phones... A WORD OF WARNING do not attempt to make phone calls with a credit card. I made four attempts; each time got an answering machine and have been charged $40+ for each attempt. I am going to query the charges when I get home. I mean $160 for about 30 seconds of talk time to a machine is bloody ridiculous.

Slovakia, No Thanks

Came up to Slovakia, crossed the border and was confronted by Bratislava. By confronted, I mean all of a sudden I saw heaps of eye watering highrise that seemed to grow out of nowhere. As I cycled closer, there were more plantations of highrise in such ugly order that I had no desire to explore the city at all. Instead I raced through, helped by the well tarmaced bike paths and my desire to escape.

Now, I am going to state this straight away, I didn't like

Slovakia at all. In general, I just wanted to get through it as soon as possible. Some mitigating circumstances may have influenced this: the Danube flooding made camping uncomfortable, not having a map or money because I didn't want to change currency, destitute villages that looked utterly devoid of hope, being chased by a couple of wild dogs (something I learned to cope with later on), getting slaughtered by mosquitoes and generally feeling uneasy around the towns. There were a lot of blokes hanging around (not uncommon in Eastern Europe) and they always seemed to be eyeing me off in a menacing way.

The one saving grace was that they have some beautiful women living there. I guess it must be a trade off – here you live in a broken country with little hope or incentive, your food is bad, infrastructure woeful, services non-existent but at least your wife is gorgeous for twenty odd years.

Don't get me wrong; as I travelled through Eastern Europe, I saw many poor towns and villages, places that belonged in the dark ages, and places where horses and oxen were more common on the road than cars and trucks. Despite all that, I never got the same feeling of hopelessness and destitution that I got from the Slovak villages.

Mum's opinion is that all the good ones (hard working people with initiative) have already fled or migrated. Me, I reckon that all life has been crushed out of them during the Soviet occupation and they are drifting tiller-less at the moment. Still, I only saw a tiny fraction of the country, so maybe it's better in other areas.

Camping was a bit of a nightmare. The mosquitoes were horrendous – due to the flooding of the Danube and for the next week and a bit I was plagued by them at dawn and dusk (when I break and make camp). Tonight was the first night of their frenzy, so it helped solidify my dislike for the country.

Wild Dogs, Vandals and Skinheads

Got chased by a wild dog which led me to carry a stick on my bike much like the cane holder that I saw on an old bike in the Deutsch Museum. The tarmac petered out and was replaced by dirt tracks and vandalised bike signs with their arrows broken off. One or two is part of the territory but four in a row over 25-odd kilometres is a bit much. I gave up on the bike path and hit the main roads but without a map and with road signs in a new language and without knowing where the crossing to Hungary was, it probably wasn't the best idea. Still, by using my compass I kept in the right general direction and arrived at Komarno which had a border crossing.

Lunched there and was accosted by gypsies. One of the kids gave me a Nazi salute with the 'Heil Hitler' salutation which I thought was a bit weird but I put it down to him thinking that I was Austrian instead of Australian. I thought that he must be a well educated gypsy kid to know that Hitler was Austrian and I didn't think that I looked particularly Neo-Nazi as I have some hair now and was obviously a cycle tourer. That mystery was resolved when I crossed the border as I saw three separate groups of skinheads with 5-10 people in them. There obviously was some Neo-Nazi meeting of sorts going on.

Still I was a bit abashed that the kid had thought that I was a skin and I thought it was even funnier when he tried to beg me for change. I have a standard reply to gypsy kids when they demand, "Gimme money."

"No, piss off."

Usually this is a cyclical conversation and is conducted with smiles, goodwill and disregard for either of our requests until I cycle off. My once soft soul has been hardened by Aboriginal and Darwin's Longrasser beggars and I only give to crippled beggars.

I visited the fort at Komarom, the biggest star fort of its time which was quite impressive if a bit run down with a very unhelpful staff. It did have an area which showed all the UNESCO areas in Hungary which was helpful for my map-less travels. Cycled along dirt paths next to the Danube until dark and camped with my retinue of mossies promising myself that I would buy repellant ASAP (stupidly unfulfilled for another week).

←→

Fairly standard day, I ended up cycling most of the way on roads as the bike path seemed to have dried up. Stopped at campground to have a night off when I found out that their tent sites were closed due to the flooding. I talked to a pleasant Dutch couple who weren't too helpful in providing alternatives.

"You could go into the hills but the wolves there are pretty savage. And I wouldn't camp on the banks as you could get washed away." I finally got away by promising them that I would camp somewhere safe although it didn't seem possible from the options they had given me. Ended up camping by a river bank.

Hungary, Cartographic Comfort

Visited Esztergom in the morning which had an inspiring basilica and plenty of interesting buildings, fortifications and monuments. Although Hungary is a relatively poor country, it seems worlds apart from its neighbour Slovakia, as it has a pride in its history and its people seem far more industrious. Soviet occupation has left its mark but that seems to be healing not scarring.

Cycling to Budapest, I met some tourers who actually had a bike map of the route so I was able to get back onto the bike path and passed through some nice villages. There was one in particular, I can't remember its name, that was chocker block full of monuments. The best was an abstract wood carving of 7 poles with crowns, 1 bigger than the rest. This monument represented the 7 chieftains, something that I want to find out more about some other time. Which reminds me, along the Danube in Austria, I passed a very pretty medium sized village with two of the best fountains I've seen (I'm a strange tourist and inevitably take photos of

fountains). The best one was an immense monument picturing either the surrender or agreement to terms between a knightly group (looked like Austrians) to a westernised Asiatic group (my best guess was the Monguls). I photographed the information board so once the photos are developed, I'll need a German translator to work it out.

Spent the rest of the day cycling into Budapest. This turned into a bit of a mission as I lost the path and had my first taste of true Eastern European driving, something I would learn more about in Serbia and Bulgaria. Finally got into the city and found an island of greenery within the Danube to escape the carbon dioxide poisoning. I think that my time cycling in Eastern Europe has probably taken a couple of years off my life.

Spent the afternoon, stuffing around trying to book an airflight which became impossible because my Visa got barred electronically and I couldn't phone the number the bank gave me because I was overseas. Gave up and sent an SOS to Mum to see if she could sort it out and went looking for some accommodation.

I then met Lucas, another cyclist from England who had travelled a similar route to me along continental Europe. We ended up getting a room together, having a few beers and trading stories.

Had lunch with Lucas (the Pom) and then we went our separate ways. I spent part of the day cycling around the many impressive buildings and monuments that are Budapest. For someone who lives in a town like Darwin where practically every building is under 30 years old, Budapest is easily the visibly oldest city I have been in (apart from Rome and other Italian cities when I was much younger) with even the most common building being well aged and engraved.

I rang Mum to see what had happened with the Visa and she was a bit non-plussed which was because the main e-mail I had sent her had bounced but she promised to get onto it.

➡ No Money: Home View and Credit Card Mixup

Although Trevelyan would ring at odd hours when he found a rural phone that worked, in addition to the blog and a sporadic e-mail link being maintained, often it was understandably difficult to find Internet access so responses would be weeks apart, We were conscious of his physical exhaustion at times and concerned that he might get rundown and be short of money since the Irish Tax Department had mislaid his refund cheque, and a replacement was not re-issued for months. He had intended using this money for the major funding of his travelling.

Finally the misdirected Irish Tax Department refund which was supposed to have been paid into his Irish bank by the authorities before he left Ireland, and which they had lost in the postal service, arrived at our Melbourne family home which was his safety back- up address. The problem was that the cheque had to be signed in person, even before being credited to HIS account and Trevelyan

was uncontactable on a bike in Eastern Europe with a mobile that didn't work.

Then came the Visa card mess up, when from rural Austria he tried to Internet book ahead his Istanbul-Melbourne ticket home and the bank cancelled his Visa card, despite there being money in the account. So he had no money, and no credit card. Eventually we sorted it by getting a 'free' emergency bank phone number for him to ring, once he rang us on a 'reverse charges collect' and by adding substitute funds after we discovered that a MR in front of his name had stopped all transactions. None of us was impressed with Irish bureaucracy or banks!

Middle of the night high anxious stuff! Blog was useful for leaving 'please ring home' messages, but unsure when he would see them.

←→

Rang Mum again and she had had some hassles with bank but had got a number that I could contact which allowed me to clear the block on the VISA. I then miraculously found an Internet café straight away in a small village and was able to book my flight – for better or worse, through sickness or anything else, I needed to be in Istanbul by the 21st September.

←→

I then went a little crazy and spent about $30 on a cycle map of Hungary which I would only use for a couple of days. I think I had been starved of cartographic comfort and I didn't have a clue how much money I had taken out (it turned out to be about $300 which got me through Hungary and

Serbia).

Escaping from Budapest limpet-like to the bike trail I now knew backwards, I began to search for a campsite. Unfortunately the trail followed a canal that was obviously prized real estate canal frontage because I didn't find a site until well after dark.

Continued until I came to an interesting border-like gate. Bold as any ignorant tourist could be (I've found that when people aren't trying to fleece you this is the best approach) armed with my detailed map, I pointed to the next town and they gave me directions and opened the gate for me. For the life of me I don't know why they had a border type gate in the middle of the country although the country south of the gate had a lot more peasantry and the number of gypsies increased dramatically. Apart from that the day was uneventful with the riding being boring at best along flat headwind inducing open roads.

Disaster then struck and I had the worst run of luck in my whole trip. Let me relive that tale...

Disastrous Potholes, Mozzies, Floods and Cows

I had bought a bottle of wine (a rare occurrence) and was cycling along a dirt path just out of Fajsz. It was getting dark but I was too close to the village to camp. I ran over a pothole, the wine fell, shattered and blew my tyre. The ensuing mosquito swarm meant that I had no time to check the tyre but instead I just swapped the tube with my spare while literally on the run to avoid the mosquitoes (still no repellant).

Back on the bike, I only got a few hundred metres before the spare blew as well because there was a gaping wound in the tyre where a piece of glass had sliced it. With no time to repair either of the tubes, I ran with bike in tow until I found a suitable campsite. Under close mosquito inspection I then pitched my tent and threw everything (myself included) inside. I then killed every mossie that had followed me. They had their revenge however, because that night a thunderstorm hit and my campsite flooded, so in the middle of the night I had to drag my tent and equipment to higher ground as the mosquitoes enjoyed Round Three.

↔

In the morning I wasn't looking forward to Round Four so I hung around in my tenting fixing the punctures, jimmying the tyre wall with gaffer tape and cooking a feed. I had just finished cooking when I heard cowbells, which were then followed by the cows. For some unknown reason, a farmer drove his cattle through the marshy wooded area where I was camped. Why he wasn't on the other side of the embankment with the open grassy fields, I'll never know. So crouched over my bowl of food (I wasn't losing that!) I prayed in my soggy tent that the cows wouldn't step on me.

Luckily, only some of the cows stepped on my tent and then only on the base, so there was no real damage. A couple even poked their heads through the fly to check me out along with the cattle dogs that smelt my food but met a string of oaths. Mate when it rains, it pours…

After that rude awakening, I threw all my wet gear together in record time and gingerly cycled into Baja. All I can say is, "Thank God for Tesco." It was the only store open because it was a Sunday but that was enough to get food, MOSQUITO REPELLANT, a new tyre and various other conveniences.

I will never criticise multinational corporations with their extended working hours again.

With all the shopping, maintenance and bovine intrusions, I didn't do much cycling today but set up camp near the Serb border to the intoxicating smell of repellant – the only day I needed it because after that the swarms subsided.

➡ *Serbian Splendour*

Crossed the Serb border after a lengthy interrogation by the guards. Harmless though, the border was quiet, they were bored and I was a rarity. In fact, I only saw two other cycle tourers in Serbia and they were in Belgrade. Stopped in Somber because in Hungary the signs had shown the name as Somber Zomber which sounded pretty good to me. Unfortunately, I was disappointed as the town had nothing of real interest, so I kept going.

Stopped in Sivac and received the first of what was to be many free coffees in Serbia, a place that I really enjoyed. That

enjoyment was not born from the maps which were mislead-
ing, nor the road signs which were worse (in some places
comical), nor the roads which in parts were horrendous but
through the hospitality I received.

I managed to get mislead (by a map this time) which
would become fairly commonplace but I found a decent
campspot hidden amongst the wheat fields – northwest
Serbia is one big farm.

With dubious precision (I wanted to be on the road that
I was on but I thought I was on another one) I entered Novi
Sad and had lunch there. Conversed with the local gypsy kids
"Gimme" and "Piss off," then onto Belgrade and the happy
experience of being on a major road along with all the
Skodas, trucks and cars that can't pass Western emission lev-
els. I had by now been desensitised to crazy drivers and
appreciated that a toot from a vehicle was generally a friend-
ly warning not the: "Get off my road" that I initially thought
it was. That and having my singlet or shirt blown over my
head by an enthusiastic bus or truck doesn't irk me like it
used to.

In one piece (physically anyway) I got into Belgrade and
started to look for accommodation. The girl at the tourist
bureau was very helpful, told me there were no hostels but
pointed me to the university for cheap accommodation. The
uni however was non-plussed until a bright spark said that
there was accommodation somewhere on a long street.
Following these general instructions I went along the street
and must have looked pretty forlorn, because a lady came to
help. She instructed me to the music students' barracks
which unfortunately was closed for renovations. The tourist
bureau was also closed now because it was quite late but by

the help of some more Good Samaritans, I found a cheap hotel and crashed there. After all the mossies and traffic, the hotel was like an oasis of luxury and I went out and had lots of fast food to celebrate.

←→

I was getting my laundry done by the hotel because they told me that there wasn't a self service anywhere but I think I was fleeced as they charged me 770 dinas – enough for me to live for a week. However, my laundry was extremely clean and I had the morning to explore Belgrade and do a blog update.

I had a look around Kalemegdan Park and the town fortifications before heading off and promptly getting lost. I already doubted the authenticity of my map after coming across various errors in it but I thought that if I stuck with the river I should be ok. That proved presumptuous because the roads ran out and I was stuck in the slums of Belgrade.

After getting some directions from a lady I ended up following a tractor trail over a couple of hills to the city dump and surprised some people by cycling through their shanties on a trail that they knew led to nowhere. I wanted to photograph the emaciated state of that shanty town but felt that it would be an invasion into someone else's pain. That and I was a bit worried about the (maybe) rabid dogs living off the tip coming to visit me.

Back onto more civilised roads and their accompanying traffic. Belgrade is in a pretty hilly locality and I slogged on to Smederevo. As I was approaching, it had all the symptoms of a run down industrial town – that is I saw a large derelict processing plant and I was thinking to myself, this could be a rough town.

I then began comparing it to Liverpool and predicting that they had a big soccer team in their local league when, I swear not a word of a lie, I came upon the biggest sport stadium that I had seen on my trip. It was also a bit run down so I vowed to get out ASAP. I stopped a cyclist for directions and we had a bit of a yarn. He asked where I was staying and when I told him that I was camping he said, "No, no, you are coming with me." It turned out that he was heading to a party in Pozarevac– a drinking dancing Serbian banquet for his mate who was about to do military service.

Doing military service in Serbia is sort of like a coming of age thing because they get paid nothing (200 dinas a month – a quarter of a hotel wash) so the victims get lots of food, drink and presents before they go. Dukic (the cyclist) and Boyan (the victim) adopted Edwardovic (me) as a guest of honor so I ate, drank and danced until dawn.

The hospitable Serbian mates –
Boyan, Damir, Edwardovic and an extra mate.

Waking up in Boyan's bed, I spent the day with Dukic and Boyan relaxing at the pool. Boyan's mother and aunt supplied us with an almost endless stream of coffee, cake ("Cake, cake, you must eat cake, I have 18 cakes, you must eat them"), and food. Boyan made me promise to stay another day as there was to be the opening ceremony for the 42nd Ljubicevo Equestrian Event and he had some photos in the photographic club display. Boyan was not only a budding triathelete (Dukic was as well) but a rockclimber, fitness freak and amateur photographer.

Hung around with Boyan and Dukic and planned the next stage of my trip with suggestions from them. We then went into town, saw the start of the ceremony, a parade (lots of gypsies on horses – they love horses), fireworks, concert (there was an exceptional Serbian band called Balkania, I think) and then went to the photographic club for the opening of the display.

I think they were trying to set me up with secretary of the club who was very cute but I promised my mother not to marry any Eastern European girls this trip. Had a great time. Most people spoke some English and if they didn't I could always grab one of the young girls to act as an interpreter. The only time things were a bit awkward was when someone would ask me: "Why did the Americans bomb us?" I would have to explain my ignorance; explain that Australia wasn't a small America and that we didn't know what happened in Eastern Europe.

Partly it was true, I knew that there had been some bombings in Serbia, but I thought it was only for a week or two and in a small area, not the 4-5 month countrywide campaign. Eventually the conversation would sway back to something else less political and the usual Serbian emotive, fun-loving demeanor would come through.

↔

A little hungover, I assured Boyan that I had to go because he was beginning his military service and I had a date to keep in Istanbul. An exceptional host to the end, he escorted me to the town limits before we parted with promises of sending me photos from the Club. In return I promised to send Oz music, photos and various other things but I had to give him something immediate in return for his hospitality, so I gave him my juggling balls.

Not interested in doing too many miles, I picked up the Danube and as advised, camped near an old Roman fort on the river.

↔

The last stretch that I rode along the Danube was very pretty, in a reasonably well-wooded valley. I was about to enter real rural Eastern Europe (East Serbia and Bulgaria) where the hills and mountains are carpeted by forest, the villages are basic and carts, bikes and motorbike relics are the main transport.

Ditching the Danube I bade farewell to flat terrain and mossie epidemics and headed into the hills. These were not well signposted and I managed to miss the major (red) and secondary (yellow) intersections before heading south along a minor road. Traffic was non existent as the road steadily crumbled away until even I was having trouble making headway. I ended up toiling away along the road until I got to Gomjane.

Rural Hospitality

Here I asked a lady for directions because after the previous road, I didn't know what to expect. She took me into the kitchen, made me coffee and then practically the whole village (or so it seemed) came through to inspect my map and work out what I was saying. After finally agreeing on a route, I set off. Half an hour later a car drove past with a couple of villagers checking I had gone the right way and to bring me some apples. Camped in the hills with my shifter handy (something I'd taken to doing recently) as I heard some wolves calling as I was setting up camp.

↔

Off again only to find that I was on the wrong route. I learnt to stick to yellow and red roads from then on. I got a good photo of a sign in Zajecar pointing in two opposite directions to get to Knjazevac. If you followed the one to the left it brought you back to the same intersection so in a way the sign was correct but only when you stopped following it.

Did my shopping in Knjazevac. Unfortunately, Tesco doesn't exist in Serbia and the shops stock very similar goods with the occasional difference. This meant that I ended up going to five different shops that all had milk and yoghurt to get meat, bread and batteries as well. Very confusing for the

visitor.

Camped in the hills, next to a very cold mountain river just off a yellow road.

Trevelyan's hospitable host family.

 *Bulgarian Brigands*

Lunch in Pirot and then across the Bulgarian border. As I was waiting through customs, a bus driver came up for a yarn and after I told him my route he went back to the other bus drivers and they brought me bottles of water. Ahhh, there's nothing more ego inflating than free drinks.

Bulgaria seemed even more peasantry than Serbia and

the signs were just as helpful. Perhaps I am not being very fair because they might have been correct but unfortunately they were written in the local Ciscern alphabet and although I had bought three maps so far (one with things to see, a proper driving map and a town map to get out of Sofia) they all had the Bulgarian names in English characters, which often bore absolutely no resemblance to what was on the sign. Some of the signs were bi-alphabetical but enough weren't, enabling me to get happily lost and to fear treading on white roads.

There was however, a cobbled road that ran fairly parallel to the main road so I followed that until it got dark.

Rode into Sofia and was initially fairly desperate about it because I saw some fountains that didn't work, which reminded me that I hadn't seen any fountains in a long time. Lots of nice sights and Sofia seemed to exude some energy even though it looked like its best days were behind it. I stopped to take a picture of a building behind a fountain when I noticed people were washing themselves and drinking from what appeared to be a holy fountain.

I followed suit and filled my water bottle. Since then I have had diarrhea. I don't blame it on the holy water though, because I used that for cooking water but still the circumstances are fairly chilling. Spent a long time trying to escape Sofia. Got lost through all three methods – following signs, map reading and asking directions. In desperation I bought a town map of Sofia and got on the path that I wanted.

Cycling along the E-8, I saw why the motorway had taken over this once main route, as the road was pothole-ridden to an amazing level between Novi Han and Vakarel. Had the rare pleasure of overtaking cars and trucks as they gingerly weaved along. I passed through some barren towns. The number of gypsies had definitely grown and the country looked pretty run down, although there did seem to be some signs of life – unlike Slovakia.

It appeared that the river I was following had flooded recently as bridges were down or carrying damage or debris, but luckily there were no mossies. Camped just shy of Belovo.

$$\leftrightarrow$$

Was buying some brekkie in Zvanicevo, I was buying more and cooking less now that meals were so cheap, which might account for the diarrhea. Then a girl came up and invited me to coffee with her father. Ahhh, free coffee. Bulgaria rose in my estimation. Rode through Pazardzik which was a pretty depressing town filled with high-rise. I nicknamed the road between it and Plovdov Whores (Hoars) Highway, as for the first time this trip I saw prostitutes flirting their wares along the road, and not just one or two. Heaps of them, which made for some exciting cycling as I politely refused all advances.

Despite its nice views, Plovdov left a bad taste in the mouth as I asked a young bloke for directions and he just arrogantly shrugged his shoulders. I'm pretty sure he didn't speak English because he didn't react to my emotionless rejoinder, "Yeah, you just don't care." Arrogance seems a social norm here as prancing fashion victims (I'm talking about the blokes) are more common than I have seen elsewhere. The women are very cute though.

Found an Internet café late at night so I camped just outside Plovdov so that I could come back tomorrow to do a big catchup.

↔

Spent all day writing blog… Finished… Tired… Need to eat.

Turkish Trials

Decided to detour through the hills as I had plenty of time to spare – ten days to get to Istanbul and only 500 odd kilometres to do. I got to Asenovgrad all ready to visit the Assen Fortress but like most things in Bulgaria; there were no directions to get there once I hit the town. I was searching my map wondering where to go when a guy on a scooter zoomed up and asked where I was going. I showed him on the map and he bade me to follow leading me to the main road out of town. He then gave me a loaf of freshly baked bread. I took that as a sign to keep going and not to worry about the fortress. The cycling was good, the weather was warm, traffic light and hills not too steep. Camped on the road to Kardzalı.

↔

Woke and decided not to go to Kardzalı so headed to Haskovo instead and was impressed by the fountains there. The traffic built up along the road to Harmanlı. Was stopped by police who were pulling everyone over around Ljubimec as a bike race (Tour de Bulgaria?) zoomed past. With a criti-

cal eye, I decided that they were going slightly faster than me so I didn't bother chasing them once they had passed.

My war on insects continued as a wasp flew into my ear and as I was fishing it out, it stung me on the cartilage. That was a bit rough! It wasn't my fault that he had flown in there. I have now decided to wear earphones all the time as a precaution.

I was hailed over by an ice-cream seller on the road out of Ljubimec. He sat me down and served me up an ice-cream. After eating it and the general small talk, I pulled out my wallet to pay and when I showed him that I only had 10 Bulgarian dollars he snatched it out of my hand.

"Hey, don't be gammon," I said, as it was obvious that he wasn't going to give me any change (the ice cream was only worth a dollar). In the end, he relented and gave me $4 change. I couldn't be bothered arguing anymore so I rode away.

 *Racing Cars*

Rode through Svilengrad which looked like one big refugee camp. In fact the towns either side of the Turkish border looked as if a war had passed through fairly recently. I saw a heap of posh sports cars flying rally colours at the border and tried to talk to a couple of them.

The three drivers I spoke to were a rich Swiss, American

and English trio and I got the definite impression that they didn't want to waste their valuable vocal chords on someone who didn't even own an engine. All I could get out of them was that they were doing a drive from Monaco to Istanbul. The Turkish drivers on the other hand had no such inhibitions and they beeped, waved and instructed me on how to clear customs ASAP. The rally drivers ended up having to pass me twice, before and after the border.

Passed through Erdine which was a great looking town. By now, I was used to Eastern driving in which 'might is right' was the mantra rather than mere rules or signs. A bike being near the bottom of that traffic food chain. Still, once you were in a town the advantage of a bike was that you were able to travel on roads or pavements, and town riding could be an exhilarating experience of dodging, weaving and beeping.

Turkish towns were in some ways prettier than western ones, the buildings had different architecture and the spires and domes from the mosques were a refreshing change from all the churches I'd passed over the last four months. Unfortunately, I had a double puncture and used the last of my patches and as the day had been pretty hot, I ended up staying at a caravan park just out of Erdine.

↔

A mostly boring day filled with cycling along the D100. Turkey from my viewpoint was one big mass of undulating hills filled with plains. Boring cycling as there were no trees and I was either climbing or descending with no flat areas so I didn't really feel like I was getting anywhere. Another puncture meant I had to call into a small town to get more patches.

Open plains also meant nowhere to camp so I waited until sunset and then camped in a deserted, half built service station with no roof. I took the chance of no tent and true to form, it rained during the night. Luckily, the rain was light so I just pulled the tent fly over me and that kept everything dry.

Istanbul not Constantinople

I woke at sunrise and broke camp to more plains, more hills and more heat. Cycling was hard work compounded by the fact that I managed to shatter one of my pedals just after I had a coffee with some textile factory security guards. This meant I had to cycle 20 kilometres on just the bar until I reached Corlu and could get it fixed. New pedals plus labour (getting the old rusted pedals off was hard work) cost me 5 million Turkish lira (or the price of a coffee at the airport in Istanbul). I then had some lunch at a café and had some of the hottest food to date. I have a suspicion that the blokes were testing me out but as I had been having chilli with most meals I passed (just).

Cycling on the D100 started to get busier and then unfortunately a large portion of my side of the highway was taken up for road works. This lead to probably the most testing cycling of the whole trip. The hills were continuous and the wind blew up to gale force and would alternate between a head and crosswind. I was sharing a very small lane with a lot of trucks and heavy vehicles and as they zoomed past either the addition or sudden lack of wind pressure meant that I had to hang on for dear life. Uphill wasn't too bad but going downhill I was bloody scared on a number of occasions.

I then met an English couple on a tandem bike and had a bit of a yarn with them. They had gone all along Northern Europe and now had seven weeks to make it back to the UK. Definitely do-able but not much time for sightseeing.

I was pretty worn out as the day dragged on so when I saw a sign for a campsite just 5 kilometres away I decided 'Why not?'

Realistically the campsite sign should have said 6 kilometres because it was about 5 kilometres horizontal and 1 kilometre vertical. I don't think I have ever sworn so much on a climb as I cursed false advertising, hills, wind and then (when my chain broke), the bike as well. I was nearly there when my chain gave out so I was able to unload and make camp before fixing it. That was when I noticed that I had managed to break my seat at some stage as well.

$$\longleftrightarrow$$

After an early morning breakneck descent, following the D100 now became more exciting as it got closer to Istanbul. There aren't many roads going into Istanbul and so the few there are, are big. The road continually widened until at one stage it was 12 lanes wide. The D100 was now a freeway in anything but name and I think the only reason it wasn't named as such was to allow vehicles that weren't usually allowed on freeways (scooters, bikes, horse drawn carts etc…)

into Istanbul.

After countless beeps, tons of exhaust fumes and numerous close calls, I finally made it to the outer city near the airport. Here I decided to catch the light rail into the centre as I didn't have a map and I wasn't even sure what the centre of town was called (Istanbul is built on a number of hills).

Five months after beginning this blog, the end was nigh... That's right, despite the best efforts of mad drivers, crazy dogs and weird and wonderful food and water, I'd managed to reach Istanbul.

Once in the centre, I bought a map, some food, and found out that there was a campground half an hour away so rode there. My initial impressions of the campground were reserved as although it was next to the sea, it looked pretty rough and was surrounded by highrise. The asking price – 10 euros a night was pretty steep as well but when they brought it down to 7 euros I was convinced. My initial reservations were well founded as it was run down, the toilets were flooded and all the running water (showers included) was salt water. Considering how I had lived for the past five months though, just having a shower was good enough for me.

Woke late and was too tired to do anything energetic. Instead I went to the local shopping mall, bought an English book, did some food shopping and then watched Cinderella Man. Cooked food, read book and had a cold salt water shower.

Cycled into town and visited the military museum as per a tip-off from my Uncle Ron. One thing that I noticed about Istanbul was the amount of security they had. Shopping malls had metal detectors, armed guards and dogs. Any building that looked important had army security complete with checkpoints and bunkered lookout posts. The military museum had army security and I had to go through two metal detectors to get in. Once I was in, I got to see the Janissary military band who was very good so I bought what I thought was a CD of the music for Dad but it turned out to be a VCD in Turkish. At least it has lots of colour and some music.

Following my map I cycled along the Golden Horn and the Bosporus, taking in the sights (and lots of smells) of Istanbul. I tried to get to the Asiatic side as there was a hill which had a good view over the European side and I was hoping to get a sunset photo. Unfortunately, I couldn't work out a way to get onto the freeway bridge and after an hour or so of cycling up hills and dead ends, I gave up.

Went into town and visited the old Galata Bridge where they were holding the Istanbul design week. I had a fair yarn to the security guy about where to leave my bike and where I'd been. He was impressed and when I went to pay the $12 entrance, he just waved me through. The display was good especially some of the practical pieces and architectural designs.

Shopping in Istanbul is bartering at its best. Normally, I'm not into bartering as I'm a pretty hopeless shopper and don't have a clue what anything is worth but I wanted to get some presents for my family, had limited money and I had a fair idea what Turkish currency was worth. Shopped for a fair while and then scored a bike box. Well, I scored an old scooter box, which I could fit my bike and all my bags in. Getting it back to the campsite took the rest of the arvo because the box couldn't be compressed and I had to carry it while walking the bike. I ended up getting the train but I was still

exhausted by the time I got to the camp.

←→

Went to the Hagia Sofia and was suitably impressed with the mosaics and detail of the church turned mosque turned museum. Unfortunately the iconic dome which has been called the 'window to heaven' by someone, lost most of its spectacular presence by the mass of scaffolding that reached to the top. The base of the scaffolding covered a full third of the mosque ground floor. I couldn't help humming the tune Stairway to Heaven although the scaffolding was also serviced by a lift. Maybe the lift was the direct access for the more pious devotees?

Continuing on the tourist bent, I then went to the Grand Bazaar and the Egyptian Markets for a bit of light shopping and a look around. Light shopping it had to be because I had only the Turkish equivalent of $65 left and out of that I had to pay $50 rent and get a taxi to the airport. I think my affluently colored skin (white) fooled most store owners and despite my protestations I was taken into a car-pet shop, supplied tea and shown a range of carpets which I agreed were lovely but unless the price was $5, they weren't going to look lovely on my walls and floors.

With no money left, I cycled up to an old cemetery where there was a good lookout at the top of the hill. There was even a coffee shop there and although I didn't have enough money for a coffee, I ended up having a chat with an American guy who had spotted my bike. It turned out that he was a street performer and would spend 9 months a year cycling around the world performing to finance his travel. Wow, just when you think that you're doing a hardcore trip you find someone who makes it pale in comparison.

From the mount, I got a good shot of the Golden Horn (the river splitting the European section) and although I would have loved to stay there until sunset to see if the river did in fact turn golden, I had a fair ride to get back and dusk was at least an hour off. I had a yarn with the campsite owner and when I told him that I wasn't religious he looked at me almost pityingly and kept saying, "Very dangerous." I'm pretty sure he wouldn't have minded me being Christian but to have no religion at all was an anathema to him. In his eyes my soul was very unfortunate to be caught up in the heathen body/mind of mine.

My last dinner in Europe was a pretty staid affair of two loaves of bread and a cup of tea.

↔

September 21st packed all my things, ate breakfast (an apple which would have to do me all day until I was on the plane) and caught a taxi to the airport. I had got the camp owner to set the price at 10 million with the taxi driver, but at the airport he tried to charge me $US10 (about 15 million). I had to laugh when he demanded it because I only had the 10 million left. Once he worked out that that was all the money I had, he smiled and bade me well. As a side note, it was only once I got to Istanbul that the Turks there tried to swindle me. In the countryside they were like anyone else and very helpful.

The trip home was a forgettable one of security scans, unpacking-packing repeated five times as my collection of bike tools and gift knife gave the security staff nightmares. In all, I managed to keep all my gear despite confiscations in

Dubai and the bike box falling to pieces.

Getting picked up by Dad at the airport was surreal as a five month cycle chapter of my life closed and I made it home in time for my mother's significant birthday!

 The End...

The final trip write up. Apart from photos which are taking a while to scan. Staying with my parents in Melbourne has reintroduced me to the multitude of comforts of Oz. Doonas, artificial lighting, flu, hot showers, deodorant, fridges, permanent lodgings, quiet cars and most importantly, clean western toilets.

The trip home jet-lagged me a bit and I was pretty worn out when I got here so I've spent the last week pottering around, walking the dog, getting a mild cold, catching up with family and friends, cleaning all my equipment and slowly scanning my photos. I finally signed my Irish tax refund cheque and got it into the system so I could repay my debts.

I hadn't realised how basically I had been living across the five months and have lost several kilos...

Kim (my sister) and I borrowed Mum's credit card and did a bit of a shopping spree so I now have more than one pair of shoes, as well as some pants and shirts that don't look like they've spent months on the trail. Settling back into suburbia, one of the things that has stuck out has been the organized partitioning of houses and the lack of people on the streets. In Eastern Europe people lived outside their houses, while here they live in them. Still, I'll be back in Darwin soon where balconies and barbies rule supreme...

 *PS*

Today, March 17 2006 (St Patrick's Day), Dublin Post Office Lost Property rang me in Darwin to say they'd discovered my lost backpack with my backup documents, photos and clothes from one year ago. They're even prepared to post it free to Darwin where I am now living. That's an Irish miracle!

↔

"It is good to have an end to journey toward; but it is the journey that matters, in the end." Ursula K. Le Guin

Starting out on the bike called Stormbringer.

Above: Irish peat farmer   /   Below: Irish recycling

Above: Loch Ness back pass
Campsites
Below: West Manchester campsite beneath freeway
Opposite top: Perenes campsite
Opposite middle: Campsite near Chouse-s-Loire
Opposite bottom: Campsite in abandoned Turkish service station

Above: Pausing for refreshment, Argen River.

Water Stops

Below: Trail flooded by the Danube.

Left: Bike sculpture

Below: Aigle – the start of the Alps

Falls

Left: Axalp waterfall

Below: Falls and
crashes

Time

Right: Deutches Museum cartography exhibit

Below: Confusing Knajazevac signposts

Above: Bike bits at the end.

Left: Trevelyan and sister Kim.

Below: Edwards family on Trevelyan's return.

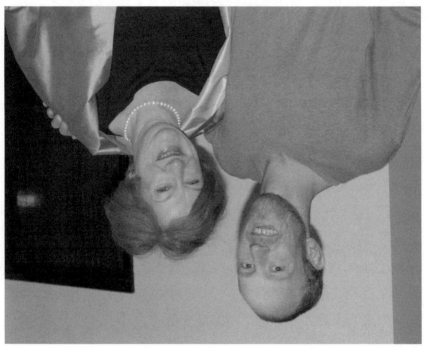

Trev and Hazel – Trevelyan made it back home for his mother's 60th
birthday, and got dressed up!

like Istanbul, Budapest or Vienna or the museums or the gorgeous European women. What a question to answer.

"Och aye, Istanbul's a long way laddie, you should fly."

"Nah, I want to see what's in between."

←→

Trevelyan Edwards was the three year old mind which inspired 'There's a Hippopotamus on Our Roof Eating Cake' (Penguin) which is 27 this year.

He is now back in Darwin at his own flat, with a bed and working toilet, but he has still got the bike for transport until he can afford a Land Cruiser, which may be some time. One day he might buy a watch.

same fears as getting lost in the Territory and it was never long before I would find a village and the only thing that was lost was a bit of time.

Time was the only thing that mattered… time to have a yarn… to gesticulate and explain that I wasn't Austrian, "Nien spreche sie Deutsche" do a skippy dance and say "Syderney" and "Melerburn" umpreen times. Time to explain that I wasn't really from Sydney but oh well, it didn't matter and by the way this coffee is great but how do you say milk in your language?

That brings me to what was the biggest highlight of the trip, that was the hospitality I received throughout the trip. I lost count of the amount of free coffees I received and friend-ly interest that was taken in my trip.

↔

Away from the common sense (if not dialect) of Scotland, the hospitaliry of Eastern Europe was second to none. Although language could be a barrier I got by on basic French, desperate German and a lot of Ocker (I didn't want to be mistaken for a Pom). There was always someone in a village who spoke some basic English and the one time there wasn't, the mayor of the town had an English speaking sister who acted as a translator on his mobile.

I've got countless stories of people going out of their way to direct me, buy me coffee and there was even a guy in Bulgaria who drove off then caught up with me half an hour later with a loaf of the local bread. Without doubt however, the most hospitable encounter I had was with a Serbian fam-ily in Pozarevac, the birthplace of Slobodan Milosevic.

Highlight? I haven't even begun talking about the cities

Trevelyan's blog was taken down, but here's an overview extract about Serbia from the ABC Perspectives radio program which was recorded but has not yet gone to air.

Solo Cyclist Cartographer

The question any traveller fears...

"So you cycled from Ireland to Istanbul. What was the highlight?"

I mean, how do you compress five months of camping, travelling, sightseeing freedom into a single highlight?

To avoid repetition, I usually answer that question with generalisations.

Sometimes I talk about the scenery – the ascetic beauty of Ireland's islands, Scotland's glens, Switzerland's Alps, France's canals, Germany's churches and Austria's fountains. Scenery is hard to describe though so other times I talk about the freedom of travelling on a bike and being able to camp wherever I could find a reclusive clearing. Preferably next to a river for washing and cooking but apart from that, I carried everything else. Waking up without a clue of where you'll be the next night except that it will be within 150km is my kind of blissful travelling.

Following local tracks and maps wasn't always a good idea though especially in Eastern Europe where I found some of the maps more of an approximation and 'road' being a very general term covering everything between tarmac and goat trails. Being a cartographer by trade, this irked my professional interest but didn't damper my wanderlust.

Who cared if all my maps were in English, while the signs were in Cyrillic? Getting lost in Europe doesn't hold the

As an author I could sympathise with his hurried entries, so I collated and edited them. Not just as a 'organising parent who was also a writer' but so that the first hand experience of cycling solo from Ireland to Istanbul could be reflected upon, later.

Cycling solo on a mountain bike and camping out, from Ireland to Istanbul, on a very limited budget is an extreme adventure, especially when bureaucratic mixups cut off the credit links.

While the blog was in progress, many bike clubs started reading it and forwarding it. Weekend cyclists related to the details of managing bike disasters like punctures, while orienteers liked the terrain details. Others liked the food details or the humorous descriptions of 'what went wrong'.

Many bloggers tend to have one track minds and talk only of one subject. Luckily this blog avoided the boredom of repetition by focusing on a different aspect for each country's entry.

Generally, the **dangers** in a blog are:

- No checking of content and any unsupported views can be spread.
- A possible channel for bigotry or propaganda.
- Inaccuracies are perpetuated.
- In the 'comments' area some inappropriate or stupid comments can be added by strangers and the blogger has no redress.
- Writing honestly in a genuine fashion which is the most effective tone means you are open to derogatory remarks which can be unfounded and unanswerable.
- Repetition.

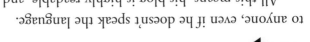
to anyone, even if he doesn't speak the language.

All this means, his blog is highly readable, and so a wide range of friends, family and an increasing number of strangers were reading his erratic instalments.

I'd encouraged him to write regardless, because the immediacy of the experience would be lost unless written close to the daily events. And frankly, not that many people cycle alone on a push bike through such varied terrain and cultures so it was a way of checking his progress. Admittedly he is tall and fit, but regardless of safety issues, memories fade rapidly once new challenges appear.

When you travel alone, and in countries where you do not speak the language, writing is a way of recording and evaluating the significance of certain experiences, when there is no travelling companion with whom to discuss daily events.

Digital photos are another record, but even if you can upload them onto your blog, rarely will you be in them if you are travelling alone.

While working in Antarctica, I'd become aware of the psychological value of writing for isolated travellers. Apart from suffering the 'Kodak poisoning' of taking many digital photos, Antarctic expeditioners tend to write in varied forms: poetry, e-mails, journals, diaries and fiction as a way of coming to terms with the significance of being isolated as winterers from March to November.

Since I had written the serendipitous 'Antarctic Writer on ice' based on my e-mails from the 2001 Antarctic expedition, which has been reprinted several times, I know how many eager readers enjoy vicarious adventure, if the writer is honest enough about the challenges. Trevelyan is very candid.

So there is some censorship, either inherent or perceived. I was amused during one of the Irish entries which related to a town with a suggestive name, when Trevelyan qualified why he was visiting a town with the name which his mates had joked about, 'but I can't go into details because my Mum reads this Blog.'

From a family perspective, it means that any comments you add to his entry can be read by anyone worldwide, for as long as the blog stays up.

And it's better not to sign the comments 'Mum'. Some mates wrote encouraging messages, sometimes in extracts which might need censoring before use in some places. Our 6 year old wrote:

Dear Uncle Trev,

Thanks for the postcard about the Little People.

Truman

Benefits include:

Dates and times. You know when entries were added. (if you can calculate the local time zones) and so that blog entry is proof he's still alive and not in a hospital or gone missing. Friends and other family can read the blog online. You don't have to forward news.

Many blogs are egocentric ramblings, published online because no-one would want to read them otherwise. Often ungrammatical, misspelt, repetitive and with no real content. Luckily 'Velyan' as he's known in our family and Trev to his mates, is an acute observer of the unconventional. Being a cartographer he analyses structures and landscape, and tends to include technical details but in a way which novices can understand. He also has a sense of humour and can talk much about 'blogging' as web logging is called.

As a frequent-travelling family but with financially chal-lenged backpackers, across the years we've been through reverse charges on Sunday nights, e-mail, phone cards and mobiles on Roam, which didn't work in Rome nor anywhere else, especially outback Northern Territory, Serbia and the Gobi Desert.

Cyber-wise, Trevelyan introduced us to the blog. Ideally he was to update it regularly and thus only have to type one entry in expensive or remote Internet kiosks, rather than multiple e-mails or letters which often vanished into cyber-space. This happens if the wrong key is pressed in response to a foreign language instruction, or the writer runs out of the local currency.

A blog is public. Anyone can read it. Even your mother.

Edwards family bloggers – Trevelyan, mother Hazel and sister Kim, who kept in touch electronically

Blogging Benefits
While Cycling Solo
from Ireland to Istanbul

published in Practically Primary 2006

Many students and educators are blogging, as a form of electronic writing.

Why?

- Provides regular writing experience
- Publishes instantly
- Shares the immediacy of experiences which would otherwise be lost
- Can be edited and reformatted into other media later
- A means of sharing offbeat or minority viewpoints or perceptions
- A fast way of keeping in touch with a broad audience.
- Networking

Apart from school use, blogging has wider educational implications.

If you have travelling offspring, colleagues overseas or relatives doing family histories, you need to find the cheapest way of staying in touch.

Until our son Trevelyan started his five month 'Quest', while cycling solo from Ireland to Istanbul, I didn't know

Hazel visiting the International Children's Book Castle
(Schloss Blutenberg) in Munich, with Trevelyan.

Munich Lions – a parent-taken shot. Usually a solo cyclist can't photograph self.

needs to be shaped on reflection to be of the greatest benefit to the participant and to the prospective audience.

That's why this book has been co-authored from the original blogging and in answer to many questions. Since Trevelyan's return we have collaborated on writing up the significance of this medium, educationally and in several articles that have been published as well as talks recorded for radio.

New forms of communication: blogging, vlogging, and podcasting are becoming the mediums we live by. Regardless of the age or geographic location of the audience, the way we get our news and vicarious experiences has changed drastically. Tolerance for radically different lifestyles only comes with broad exposure across international boundaries and the ability to distinguish between opinion, fact and propaganda.

That's why blogging matters, at present. In the future it may be other as yet undiscovered formats of ideas transmission. But evaluation will still be important.

The curiosity and observation skills to find the truth of situations and personalities, as well as being willing to become participant-observers and try new experiences, is vital for a writer in any medium and from any generation.

⬅ Blogging Bicycology

Having a middle name like Quest was a bit of an embarrassment to Trevelyan... until he spent the five months cycling from Ireland to Istanbul. That became a bit of a Quest, and a useful name for his bike blog, scribbled in Internet cafés. The media choice of blogging to record his bike quest is significant as new technology for families and friends who wish to keep in touch internationally.

For a family, it's reassuring to know that there are electronic connections, mobile, e-mail and blogging: even if they are belated back-ups, through different time and language zones or occasionally off the map or lost in a postal system! Since it's impossible for a person to do everything in a lifetime, reading from another's perspective is a secondhand or vicarious way of experiencing others' lives. Blogging is immediate. Electronically it is a way of keeping touch when travelling friends are spread across the world.

However, unless the significance of an activity is recorded, that experience can be lost by the participant and by possible readers. A solo traveller needs to re-write, on reflection about the significance of his cycling quest, so that the instant blog notes can become a more philosophical but quirky analysis of the universality of strangers' kindnesses as well as the ignorance and prejudice of a few bigots. Experience

CYCLING SOLO

On Re-flection:
Blogging Bicycology

Hazel Edwards and Trevelyan Quest Edwards